i Think: Reading

Novel Elements

by Sharon Coletti and Kendra Corr

© InspirEd Educators, Inc.   Atlanta, Georgia

** It is the goal of InspirEd Educators to create instructional materials that are interesting, engaging, and challenging. Our student-centered approach incorporates both content and skills, placing particular emphasis on reading, writing, vocabulary development, and critical and creative thinking in the content areas.

Edited by Amy Hellen

Cover graphics by Sharon Coletti and Print1 Direct

Copyright © 2009 by InspirEd Educators, Inc.

ISBN # 978-1-933558-81-3

** FOR INDIVIDUAL TEACHER / PARENT USE **

All rights reserved. It is unlawful to reproduce all or part of this publication without prior written permission from the publisher. **Student pages only** (handouts and / or transparencies) may be photocopied or created for individual teacher or parent use. It is a breach of copyright to reproduce part or whole of this publication for any other purposes. Violators will be prosecuted in accordance with United States copyright law.

Printed in the United States of America

About InspirEd Educators

InspirEd Educators was founded in 2000 by author Sharon Coletti. Our mission is to provide interesting, student-centered, and thought-provoking instructional materials. To accomplish this, we design lesson plans with research-based content information presented in various ways and used as the vehicle for developing critical and creative thinking, reading, writing, collaboration, problem-solving, and other necessary and enduring skills. By requiring students to THINK, our lessons ensure FAR greater retention than simple memorization of facts!

Initially our company offered large, comprehensive, multi-disciplinary social studies curricula. Then in 2008 we joined forces with another small company and author, Kendra Corr, and launched a second line of thematic units, many excerpted and adapted from our original products. Now we are adding additional product lines (such as Language Arts) and authors.

Our flexible and affordable resources are ideal for individual, small, or large-group instruction. We hope you will find our company's unique approach valuable and that we can serve you again in the near future. If you are interested in our other offerings, you can find information on our main website at **www.inspirededucators.com**.

InspirEd Educators materials provide engaging lesson plans that vary daily and include:

- Lesson-specific Springboards (warm-ups)
- Writing Activities
- Critical and creative thinking
- Problem-solving
- Test-taking skill development
- Primary source analyses (DBQ's)
- Multiple perspectives
- Graphic analyses
- Fascinating readings
- Simulations
- Story-telling
- Practical use of technology
- Debates
- Plays
- Research
- Graphic organizers
- AND SO MUCH MORE!!!!!

Thank you for choosing our units,
Sharon Coletti and Kendra Corr
InspirEd Educators

©InspirEd Educators, Inc.

Tips for Teaching with InspirEd Educators Units

- Before beginning the unit, take time to look through the Objectives and lessons. This will give you a chance to think about what you want to emphasize and decide upon any modifications, connections, or extensions you'd like to include.

- Give your student(s) the Objective worksheet at the beginning of the unit study. The Objectives serve as an outline of the content to be covered and provide a means to review information. Have the student(s) define the vocabulary terms as they progress through the lessons and thoroughly answer the essential questions. You can review their responses as you go along or wait and check everything as a test review. It is important that your student(s) have some opportunity to receive feedback on their Objective answers, since assessments provided at the end of the unit are based on these.

- Read through each lesson's materials before beginning. This will help you better understand lesson concepts; decide when and how to present the vocabulary and prepare the handouts (or transparencies) you will need.

- "Terms to know" can be introduced at the beginning of lessons or reviewed at the end, unless specified otherwise. (In a few instances the intent is for students to discover the meanings of the terms.)

- Look over what we have given you and use whatever you feel your student(s) need. Suggestions are sometimes offered for enrichment, but feel free to use any lesson as a jumping off point to pursue other topics of interest.

- Our materials are intended to prompt discussion. Often students' answers may vary, but it's important that they be able to substantiate their opinions and ideas with facts. Let the discussion flow!

- Note that differentiated assessments are provided at the end of the unit. Feel free to use any of these as appropriate; cut-and-paste to revise, or create your own tests as desired.

- For additional information and research sites refer to the Resource Section in the back of the unit.

- InspirEd Educators units are all about thinking and creativity, so allow yourself the freedom to adapt the materials as you see fit. Our goal is to provide a springboard for you to jump from in your teaching and your student(s)' learning.

- ENJOY! We at InspirEd Educators truly believe that teaching and learning should be enjoyable, so we do our best to make our lessons interesting and varied. We want you and your student(s) to love learning!

4   ©InspirEd Educators, Inc.

Table of Contents

Objectives (terms, questions and answers) … page 6

The Good Book (reading a novel) … page 8

Sorting Things Out (genres) … page 12

Author-ity on the Subject (purpose and motivation) … page 16

Of "Good" Character (characterization) … page 21

Round and Around (round and flat characters) … page 25

The Players (character roles) … page 30

From the Horse's Mouth (dialogue) … page 34

Tellers of Tales (point of view) … page 38

Putting Up a Fight (conflict) … page 43

Plotting (plot) … page 47

Look Around (setting) … page 52

The Power of Words (imagery) … page 57

A Way with Words (figurative language) … page 61

In a Good Mood? (mood) … page 65

It Is What It Is, Or Is It? (symbolism) … page 69

Get the Message? (theme) … page 74

Isn't It Ironic? (irony) … page 78

Tying Up Loose Ends (novel project) … page 86

Reviewing Terms (vocabulary puzzle) … page 90

Differentiated Content and Skills Assessments
(A – modified; B – average; C – accelerated) … page 92

Resources (bibliography) … page 97

©InspirEd Educators, Inc.

Novels Objectives

Vocabulary - Be able to define and use the following terms:

- novel
- fiction
- matrix
- genre
- purpose
- motivation
- biography
- milestone
- character
- trait
- characterization
- culture
- protagonist
- antagonist
- foil
- mentor
- archetype
- dialogue
- narrator
- first person
- third person
- conflict
- plot

- exposition
- inciting force
- rising action
- climax
- falling action
- resolution
- foreshadowing
- setting
- imagery
- sensory
- alliteration
- assonance
- simile
- metaphor
- idiom
- onomatopoeia
- mood
- symbol
- context
- theme
- improvisation
- irony
- review

Fully answer the following questions.

1. Explain what a novel is and describe some common genres.
2. Explain how an author's purpose and motivation can affect a story.
3. Explain how authors create and bring characters to life.
4. Describe how point of view can affect a story.
5. Describe the four types of conflict and explain how they enhance a story.
6. Describe the elements of plot.
7. Explain the importance of setting and mood.
8. Explain how symbolism and theme are used in novels.
9. Describe the different types of irony and explain why they are used.

Novels Objectives - Answers and Explanations

Vocabulary - Be able to define and use the following terms:
Definitions for terms are provided in the lessons in which they are introduced.

Fully answer the following questions:

1. *Novels are fictional stories usually divided into chapters. Most novels can be categorized by types called genres such as romance, science fiction, or mystery.*

2. *The background and life experiences of an author can not only affect what he/she chooses to write about, but the way a story is told.*

3. *Authors can introduce characters in a variety of ways: describing their physical attributes, personality traits, or their actions. Some characters are essential to the story; these should be "round" or complex and detailed, while others are "flat" or simple and not integral to the story. Characters play differing roles. Protagonists are among the main characters, opposed by an antagonist which can either be another person or situation. Foils, or sidekicks and mentors who guide protagonist also serve to reveal information about him/her. Dialogue can also be useful in character development.*

4. *Stories can be told in the first or third person. In the first person point-of-view the narrator (or storyteller) is a character in the story. These accounts tend to be more personal, but can be biased, as opposed to third-person point of view, in which the storyteller is an outside observer, who may know the thoughts of others.*

5. *Conflict can arise in several ways: man vs. man pits the main character against another person; man vs. nature has the protagonist challenged by a natural disaster or other environmental factor; man vs. society deals with problems resulting from a government or bigger force's actions; and man vs. self details a personal and internal struggle. Conflict is important because it is the basis for story plots.*

6. *Plot, the main series of events in a story, unfolds in stages. It begins with exposition, the story background and introduction of the characters. An inciting force then occurs, triggering the story's conflict. The rising action refers to the events leading to the climax, or high point in the story. Then falling action leads to the resolution of the conflict, or how things work out in the end. In addition to these stages, authors can use foreshadowing, providing clues to events yet to come to peak reader interest and increase tension.*

7. *Setting is the time, situation, and circumstances surrounding a story. It allows the reader to picture where the story takes place and experience what it would be like. A good setting is created by using imagery, or descriptive wording, and figurative language such as similes, metaphors, and onomatopoeia. Mood also contributes to setting by establishing the "feel" of the story for the reader.*

8. *Authors use symbolism to attach deeper meaning to objects, people, or places. Themes, such as the triumph of good over evil, also allow readers to "take more" from a book than is obvious. Themes are the deeper meanings of stories.*

9. *Irony can be verbal, when what is said is the opposite of what is meant; situational is when something completely unexpected occurs; or dramatic in which case the reader knows what will happen but the characters in the story do not. Irony can add humor, unexpected twists, or tension to a story.*

©InspirEd Educators, Inc.

The Good Book

Springboard:
Students should complete "Take Your Pick."
(Answers will vary but should spark discussion.)

Objective: The student will be able to explain his/her selection process for choosing a book to read.

Materials: Take Your Pick (Springboard handout)
Predicting the Future (handout)
A Novel "Matrix" (handout)

Terms to know: **novel** - a fictional storybook divided into chapters
fiction - story about imaginary people and events
matrix - a rectangular array of elements (often, but not always mathematical)

Procedure:
- **NOTE:** Arrange ahead of time for the student(s) to go to the library or choose a novel to read by some other means.
- After reviewing the Springboard, explain that <u>in this unit the student(s) will be studying novels</u> (review terms) <u>and, along with learning about novels in general, they will be reading one as they progress through the unit</u>.
- At this point have the student(s) select a novel (or more) to read in conjunction with their novel study. Once book(s) are chosen, have the student(s) explain what led them to select the novel(s) they did. *(Answers will vary.)*
- Distribute the "Predicting the Future" handout and have the student(s) use their chosen or assigned novel to complete the handout.
- Have them share their predictions and discuss.
- Then distribute the "A Novel 'Matrix'" handout and review the directions. Explain that <u>the organizer will help the student(s) keep track of important events, people, problems, etc. in their story, as well as helping to analyze the novel in light of what they learn in this unit</u>. (**NOTE:** This and other handouts about the chosen novel should be completed as directed, and all should be retained for use in the final project.)
- Allot any remaining time for the student(s) to begin reading their book(s).

Take Your Pick

DIRECTIONS: Browse this list of well-known novels and answer the questions below.

Gone With the Wind	Animal Farm
Catcher in the Rye	Slaughterhouse Five
Lord of the Rings	Lord of the Flies
The Great Gatsby	Night
The Call of the Wild	Fahrenheit 451
Sophie's Choice	My Sister's Keeper
Don Quixote	Moby Dick
The Scarlett Letter	Jane Eyre
Uncle Tom's Cabin	Dracula
The Stranger	2001 A Space Odyssey
Snow Falling on Cedars	To Kill a Mockingbird
White Oleander	Angela's Ashes
The DaVinci Code	The Notebook
Life of Pi	Twilight
A Separate Peace	She's Come Undone
Cry the Beloved Country	Beloved
Harry Potter and the Goblet of Fire	The Lovely Bones
The Godfather	The Sun Also Rises
The Grapes of Wrath	Ulysses
Their Eyes Were Watching God	The World According to Garp

Choose one title from the list that you have heard of and might want to read and explain why it sounds interesting to you. _____
_____
_____
_____

Other than looking at titles, what other methods do you use to find a book you want to read? _____
_____
_____
_____
_____
_____

©InspirEd Educators, Inc.

Predicting the Future

Read the title of the book. Predict what you think the story is going to be about. _____
_____
_____
_____
_____

What makes you think you might like this story? _____
_____
_____
_____
_____

Flip to the table of contents and scan the chapter titles. What can you predict based on this information? _____
_____
_____
_____
_____
_____

Read the first two pages of the book. Do you want to change any original predictions based on the introduction? Explain. _____
_____
_____
_____
_____
_____

Write three questions that you predict will be answered by the end of the book.
1. _____
_____
2. _____
_____
3. _____
_____

10 ©InspirEd Educators, Inc.

A Novel "MATRIX"

DIRECTIONS: As you read, record the information in the chart from each chapter. Request additional "Matrix" forms as needed.

Chapter	Most Important Event, etc.	Notes

©InspirEd Educators, Inc.

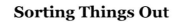

Sorting Things Out

Springboard:
Students should complete "Showing Favoritism?"
(Answers may vary and should, hopefully, spark discussion.)

Objective: The student will be able to describe several examples of novel genres.

Materials: Showing Favoritism? (Springboard handout)
Book-Browsing (handout)
Generalizing Genres (handout)

Terms to know: **genre** - type or category, as of written works

Procedure:

- After reviewing the Springboard, explain that *it is common for people to read novels of similar types, or genres* (review term). Go on to explain that *in this lesson the student(s) will learn about some common genres of novels*.
- Distribute "Book-Browsing." Have the student(s) work individually, in pairs, or small groups using Internet resources, including an online book store to complete the handout. (**NOTE**: www.amazon.com is a great resource for this activity since the site can be searched by genre.)
- Have them share their findings and discuss any books they found that they might like to read and why.
- Distribute "Generalizing Genres." Have the student(s) use what they have learned about the various genres of novels to complete an outline.
- Then have them share and explain their outlines. *(Answers will vary but information should be organized logically based on student research.)* During the discussion have the student(s) try to identify the genre of the novel they are currently reading and share their ideas. (**NOTE:** If a student cannot determine the genre, some research should be conducted to find out.)
- **EXTENSION:** Have the student(s) use their outlines to write a persuasive paragraph explaining why their favorite genre is so good. They should, of course, use details from the outline in their paragraph. They should then share their writing.

12   ©InspirEd Educators, Inc.

Showing Favoritism?

DIRECTIONS: Think of three novels you have read and enjoyed, preferably your three favorite, and answer the questions below.

1. **Title #1:** _____

   Write a sentence telling what the book is about. _____
   _____
   _____

   What did you like about this book? _____
   _____
   _____

2. **Title #2:** _____

   Write a sentence telling what the book is about. _____
   _____
   _____

   What did you like about this book? _____
   _____
   _____

3. **Title #3:** _____

   Write a sentence telling what the book is about. _____
   _____
   _____

   What did you like about this book? _____
   _____
   _____

What, if anything, do your three novels have in common? _____
_____
_____

Often people choose to read novels that are similar. Why do you think this is so?
_____
_____
_____
_____

©InspirEd Educators, Inc.

BOOK-BROWSING

DIRECTIONS: Use Internet sites including online bookstores to find information examples of novels that "fit" each of the genres listed. Then answer the questions below.

Genre	Story Characteristics of the Genre	Example
Mystery		
Romance		
Science Fiction		
Historical Fiction		
Fantasy		
Action-Adventure		
Western		

Brainstorm a list of some other genres of novels. _____

_____

_____

_____

Which genres are your favorites? Why? _____

_____

_____

_____

How could knowing a book's genre help you understand the story? _____

_____

_____

_____

14   ©InspirEd Educators, Inc.

Generalizing Genres

DIRECTIONS: Use information from the chart and your own research to create an outline describing your two favorite genres of novels. Include enough details and/or examples so someone with no knowledge of the topic could understand it.

I. Genre One: _____
   A. Description
      1. _____
      2. _____
      3. _____
   B. Characteristics
      1. _____
      2. _____
      3. _____
   C. Examples and explanations of how each fits the genre
      1. _____
         a. _____
         b. _____
      2. _____
         a. _____
         b. _____
      3. _____
         a. _____
         b. _____

I. Genre Two: _____
   A. Description
      1. _____
      2. _____
      3. _____
   B. Characteristics
      1. _____
      2. _____
      3. _____
   C. Examples and explanations of how each fits the genre
      1. _____
         a. _____
         b. _____
      2. _____
         a. _____
         b. _____
      3. _____
         a. _____
         b. _____

©InspirEd Educators, Inc.

Author-ity on the Subject

Springboard:
Students should complete "Who Wrote It & Why?"

Objective: The student will be able to explain how an author's purpose and motivation can affect a story.

Materials: Who Wrote It & Why? (Springboard handout)
About An Author (handout)
Writer & Writing (handout)

Terms to Know: **purpose** - the intention of a writer
motivation - background, interests, experiences, concerns, etc. that guide a writer's work (or a character's actions within a work)
biography – information about a person's life; dates, family, background, etc.
milestone - turning point in a person's life

Procedure:

- While reviewing the Springboard, explain that *the purpose of a piece of writing is not the only thing that an author considers when writing a novel. The author's background and experiences also can greatly influence his/her work*. Go on to explain *that in this lesson the student(s) will research an author to analyze how his/her life experiences impact a novel*. (**NOTE**: Student(s) can either research the author who wrote the book they're currently reading, or another writer of other books they have read in the past.)

- Distribute "About an Author" and have the student(s) use the Internet to complete the note-taking form.
- Then hand out "Writer & Writing" and have the student(s) write a passage as directed.
- Have the student(s) share and compare their works and discuss.

WHO WROTE IT & WHY?

The school should ban the use of cell phones during the school day. First, cell phones can be disruptive. Students are supposed to have their phones on silent mode during class, but they often forget to set them, causing teachers to have to stop their lessons when a phone rings. Secondly, cell phones can be used to cheat. Students from one class can text answers to tests or other assignments to their friends, or use the Internet function to look up answers, even on tests! For these reasons students should no longer be allowed to have cell phones in their possession during the school day.

What is the author's purpose in writing this passage? How do you know?

Who do you think might have written this passage? Why?

Polly's Pet Palace is sponsoring a pet adoption day this Sunday, October 24. Stop by and see many breeds of cats and dogs in all sizes and colors! All animals up for adoption have been spayed or neutered and are current on all immunizations. Anyone interested in adopting can also come inside the Pet Palace for special sales and offers on everything needed for the newest member of the family!

What is the author's purpose in writing this passage? How do you know?

Who do you think might have written this passage? Why?

A man decides to learn how to skydive. After months of instruction and tandem dives he finally takes his first solo jump, but when he pulls the cord to open his chute, it doesn't work. Panicking, he tries his emergency chute, which also fails. As he plummets towards the ground, he sees a man rising towards him in the air. Confused but terrified of the deadly fall, he calls to the other man "Buddy, do you know anything about parachutes?" The other man who looks equally terrified responds, "No, but do you happen to know anything about lighting a gas grill?"

What is the author's purpose in writing this passage? How do you know?

Who do you think might have written this passage? Why?

©InspirEd Educators, Inc.   17

WHO WROTE IT & WHY? SUGGESTIONS FOR ANSWERS

The school should ban the use of cell phones during the school day. First, cell phones can be disruptive. Students are supposed to have their phones on silent mode during class, but they often forget to set them, causing teachers to have to stop their lessons when a phone rings. Secondly, cell phones can be used to cheat. Students from one class can text answers to tests or other assignments to their friends, or use the Internet function to look up answers, even on tests! For these reasons students should no longer be allowed to have cell phones in their possession during the school day.

What is the author's purpose in writing this passage? How do you know? ***This piece of writing is meant to <u>persuade</u> the reader to think as the author does. The author states and justifies an opinion to gain support for his/her viewpoint and to get the school authorities to change the cell phone rule.***

Who do you think might have written this passage? Why? ***Answers may vary; the writer could be a student, parent, or teacher. The reasons to ban cell phones would be those of someone who disagrees with the existing policy and wants it changed.***

Polly's Pet Palace is sponsoring a pet adoption day this Sunday, October 24. Stop by and see many breeds of cats and dogs in all sizes and colors! All animals up for adoption have been spayed or neutered and are current on all immunizations. Anyone interested in adopting can also come inside the Pet Palace for special sales and offers on everything needed for the newest member of the family!

What is the author's purpose in writing this passage? How do you know? ***This piece of writing is meant to <u>inform</u> the reader about a pet adoption event. The passage is informational; relevant dates, times, procedures, etc. are all provided.***

Who do you think might have written this passage? Why? ***Answers may vary; the writer is likely someone employed by or otherwise involved with the pet store or a charity working with the store in hosting the giveaway. The writer is very knowledgeable about the details of the event.***

A man decides to learn how to skydive. After months of instruction and tandem dives he finally takes his first solo jump, but when he pulls the cord to open his chute, it doesn't work. Panicking, he tries his emergency chute, which also fails. As he plummets towards the ground, he sees a man rising towards him in the air. Confused but terrified of the deadly fall, he calls to the other man "Buddy, do you know anything about parachutes?" The other man who looks equally terrified responds, "No, but do you happen to know anything about lighting a gas grill?"

What is the author's purpose in writing this passage? How do you know? ***The writer's purpose is to <u>entertain</u>. There is little other value to the piece other than being a funny story to make the reader laugh.***

Who do you think might have written this passage? Why? ***Answers may vary; the writer could be anyone because there is no direct involvement to the story.***

©InspirEd Educators, Inc.

About an Author

DIRECTIONS: Research an author to fill in the organizer and answer the question below.

Author: _____

Basic Biography:

Milestones and Accomplishments:

Famous Works:

What, if any, connections did you find between the life of the author and his/her work?

_____
_____
_____
_____
_____
_____
_____
_____
_____

©InspirEd Educators, Inc.

Writer & Writing

DIRECTIONS: Write a persuasive piece, a biographical sketch, or a story about the author you researched. Be sure to plan ahead to decide what your purpose will be: to persuade, inform, or entertain the reader. You can write about the author's life, work, or both.

Of "Good" Character

Springboard:
    Students should follow the directions to complete "Who Are They?"
    (Descriptions may vary.)

Objective: The student will be able to describe a character based on an author's introduction and development.

Materials: Who Are They? (Springboard handout)
                      It's Alive! (handout)
                      Getting to Know... (handout)

Terms to know: **character** - person or other creature in a story
                          trait - quality that can be seen (eye color, height, etc.)
                          and those that are not visible (stubbornness, shyness,
                          intelligence, etc.)

Procedure:

• After allowing time for the student(s) to share their character descriptions, explain that *the way an author describes characters is very important to the story*.

• Distribute "It's Alive!" and explain that *an author's job in describing characters is to "introduce them," help the reader "get to know" them*. Review the directions and have the student(s) read the excerpt from <u>The Bean Trees</u> and write a character description AS THEY understand the character, based upon the brief description read. (**FYI:** This except is basically all there is about that character; however the child becomes a main character in the story).

• Have the student(s) read / compare their character descriptions and explain their ideas based on the information in the excerpt. Have them also share any other understandings they may have about her that they didn't include and explain why not.

• Hand out "Getting to Know..." and have the student(s) answer the questions in the box about a character in the novel(s) they are reading and share their ideas.

• Then as you progress through the unit, refer back to this activity every four or five days and have the student(s) record and share how their character is developing.

©InspirEd Educators, Inc.   21

WHO ARE THEY?

DIRECTIONS: Study each picture and describe the people in the space to the side. Give them names, if you'd like, and include both physical and personality traits in your descriptions.

DIRECTIONS: Read the novel excerpt and highlight ways the author helps the reader understand the character described. Then write one or two paragraphs describing the character as you "see" her. Include both physical features and what you infer about the woman's personality, attitudes, life situation, feelings, etc. Remember, there is NO RIGHT ANSWER! Simply write what YOU THINK based on the information provided!

"I noticed another woman in the bar sitting at one of the tables near the back. She was a round woman, not too old, wrapped in a blanket. It was not an Indian blanket but a plain pink wool blanket with a satin band sewed on the edge ... Her hair lay across her shoulders in a pair of skinny, lifeless plaits. She was not eating or drinking, but fairly often she would glance up at the two men, or maybe just one of them. I couldn't really tell. The way she looked at them made me feel like if I had better sense I'd be scared...

... I jumped when she pecked on the windshield. It was the round woman in the blanket.

'No thanks,' I said. I thought she wanted to wash the windshield, but instead she went around to the other side and opened the door. 'You need a lift someplace?' I asked her.

Her body, her face, and her eyes were all round. She was someone you could have drawn a picture of by tracing around dimes and quarters and jar tops. She opened up the blanket and took out something alive. It was a child. She wrapped her blanket around and around it until it became a round bundle with a head. The she set this bundle down on the seat of my car.

'Take this baby,' she said."

Excerpt by Barbara Kingsolver from <u>The Bean Trees</u>, Harper Perennial, 1998.

GETTING TO KNOW

CHARACTER: _____

NOVEL: _____

By this time in your reading, you should have been introduced to at least one character. Choose one and tell what you think of him/her.

_____

_____

_____

_____

_____

_____

How did the author introduce this character? Do you think he/she made the character clear? Explain. _____

_____

_____

_____

_____

_____

_____

_____

_____

_____

As you progress through the book, jot notes about how the character changes, your thoughts on the character, and the way the author develops him/her. _____

_____

_____

_____

_____

_____

_____

_____

_____

24   ©InspirEd Educators, Inc.

Round and Around

Springboard:
Students should read "Round and Flat" and answer the questions.
(Answers will vary and should reflect passage information.)

Objective: The student will be able to explain the differences between flat and round characters and the amount of detail afforded each.

Materials:
Round and Flat (Springboard handout)
Culturally Speaking (2-page handout)
Snooping in Characters' Stuff (handout)

Terms to know:
characterization - the way authors develop characters in writing
culture - relating to excellence in the arts and literature

Procedure:

- After discussion of the Springboard, explain that *in this lesson the student(s) will learn more about round and flat characters*.
- Distribute the "Culturally Speaking" handouts. **For group instruction** either have three student(s) perform the skit or have them work in threes to read it together. **For individualized instruction** have the student read the skit or read it together, bringing in a third reader if possible.
- Then distribute the "Snooping in Characters' Stuff" and have them try to fill in the handout. The student(s) should complete this as a media center activity, having them find books with such characters. If media access is not available, they can brainstorm to complete as much of the form as they can.
- Have them share their ideas and discuss. *(Answers may vary. Some possibilities include: Dorothy's dog; Tarzan's vines; Huck Finn's and Tom Sawyer's raft; etc.)*

©InspirEd Educators, Inc.

25

ROUND and FLAT

In a novel a reader will usually "meet" several if not hundreds of characters. Some may appear once; have a chance encounter with another character, and are never seen or heard from again. Others are almost constantly involved in the events of the story. These two types of characters are often referred to as flat and round.

Whether a character is one or the other depends upon two factors: how important the character is to the story and how well the character is developed. And these two factors are very closely related. Flat characters are simple, do what they need to do, and fade into the background of the story. The purpose of a flat character is usually to provide details about one of the main characters, allowing him/her to show kindness to a stranger, jealousy, or some other trait. A flat character could be described in a sentence or two.

On the other hand the reader really gets to know and understand round characters. They are more clearly described and the author allows the reader to learn about their feelings, thoughts, deeds, and misdeeds. Good round characters are complex and many-sided, so to fully describe one would take paragraphs or a whole essay.

Novels generally give the author enough time and pages to really dive into characterization. This is why novels can have many characters, and all can intertwine in others' lives. In good fiction each character is developed according to his/her role in the story and vice versa. The reader should have feelings for or against each of the round characters, helping the story flow and become more engaging.

Give an example of a flat character in a book or movie. Briefly tell what makes him/her flat. _____

_____

_____

Give an example of a round character in a book or movie, and explain what makes that character round. _____

_____

_____

_____

_____

_____

_____

_____

_____

Culturally Speaking®

Characters:
Snalb B. Host
Ann Awthore
A. Payne Turr
(Audience - others)

The three characters are seated facing the audience.

Host - Good evening, Ladies and Gentlemen. Welcome to our weekly discussion of all things cultural. Tonight our topic of conversation is characterization, round and flat characters if you will.

As our guests this evening, we are quite honored to have with us two cultural icons of our day, Ann Awthore and A. Payne Turr. *(soft applause; guests nod their heads to the audience)* Mr. Turr, I should like to begin by asking you a question.

Payne - Of course, but please, call me Payne.

Host - Certainly, Payne. You are a portrait painter, is that correct?

Payne - It is, however my work differs from others in that I always include backgrounds in my paintings.

Host - Oh, in the style of the great Leonardo da Vinci?

Payne - Indeed. My work is frequently compared to the master. As I was saying, I place great store in having clear backgrounds, though not terribly detailed -- much like da Vinci as you say.

Host - I should think this an apt time to bring Ms. Awthore into the discussion.

Ann – Call me Ann, please. And, yes, I would very much like to comment upon what Payne was saying. As a writer I, too, must decide how much detail to include in my books. Much as in painting, the characters closest to the reader, those the reader comes to well know, are far more detailed than those who provide the background.

Payne - Indeed, what we refer to as foreground and background…

Ann - We name round and flat characters.

Host - Ah alas, our topic for the evening! What would you say is the main difference between the two? Painting and writing, I mean. Developing the details of the characters?

Ann - I would say a main difference is why we add details as we do. I decide upon my round and flat characters based upon the story and the importance each holds.

©InspirEd Educators, Inc.

Payne - For me it's a practical matter. Since my work entails painting people who are paying me to do so, they are the focus of my paintings and the details are theirs -- or at least what the subjects like to think are their details. Good skin, dark, shiny hair, that sort of thing. The subject is painted in the foreground in great detail, and the background far less so.

Ann - Exactly my point, a painter adds details based on reality or hopes thereof. In a novel the details are those the author wants to provide. It is the author's decision to decide upon both the story and whom the characters in it will be.

Payne - That is a lovely creative outlet! Can you just create characters at will?

Ann - I do that to a point. Then as the story develops I may find that one character is less needed and edit that one into the background. Once the story is clear, I must ensure that the main characters are fully round and those who merely contribute to developing the main characters are flat.

Payne - I know there are times when I decide I need more detail in part of a painting because of light or a mirror reflection or something else of that nature. Then I may go back into a painting and add detail. Do you ever find yourself doing that?

Ann - Oh, of course. Until complete, a novel is a work in progress. And character development is a very important part of that progress.

Payne - Yet unlike me, your details cannot only be what is seen.

Ann - Oh, no! I can reveal much about a character by what he or she does or thinks.

Payne - I know that sometimes I will add details to a painting to show my subjects loves or skills. I might include a family photo on a desk, a book if my subject is a scholar, a framed ski scene if that is a hobby…

Host - Do writers add items as well?

Ann - Oh, yes! Quite often! It is actually common for round characters to have some type of prop that helps us understand them, know what's important to them, much like in Payne's work. Who would Robin Hood be without his bow and arrows?

Payne - Or Dracula without his cape and coffin? The grim reaper without his staff…

Ann - Yes, many of the world's great characters have items they are known for.

Host - And that point I'm afraid will have to be our final comment this evening. I truly hope our viewers have found this discussion of characters interesting. Before we end, I should like to thank our two guest for sharing their time with us this evening *(soft applause)* and as always, thank Public Broadcasting for airing our intellectual conversation. And last but surely not least, many thanks to our viewers and audience for their fine taste. Good night.

Snooping in Character's Stuff

DIRECTIONS: Think of examples from the novel you're reading or other books, of characters that are somewhat or completely defined by the objects around them in the story. In each case tell what the object is and how it helps shape the character associated with it.

Character	Object(s)	How Contributes to Characterization

©InspirEd Educators, Inc.

The Players

Springboard:
Students should read the "Who's Who?" story and answer the questions.
(Of those characters described: Oliver is the protagonist, Fagin the antagonist, the Artful Dodger is the foil, and Mr. Brownlow is the mentor.)

Objective: The student will be able to describe the main character roles in novels.

Materials: Who's Who? (Springboard handout)
Fill 'Em Up! (handout)
By the Book (handout)

Terms to know: **protagonist** - main character in a story
antagonist - person in the story who opposes protagonist (or thing)
foil - sidekick or friend of the protagonist
mentor - a good character who guides the protagonist
archetype - character that follows a certain pattern of behaviors (may be a flat or round character)

Procedure:
- After reviewing the Springboard, explain that <u>all stories must have a protagonist and antagonist to create action and tension. (**NOTE** that in some cases the latter can also be a THING such as the industrial and poorhouse system in Oliver Twist.) In addition to these, novels also have other fleshed out characters that fit into certain archetypes</u> (review terms) <u>such as the foil and mentor (others include the mother, child, traitor, shrew, hero, outcast, etc.).</u>
- Distribute "Fill 'Em Up!" **For group instruction** students should be grouped into teams of four to five. Give a time limit (about 10 minutes is good), and have the teams brainstorm to fill as many spaces as they can with names from books, movies, and television shows. **For individual instruction** the student and parent/instructor should complete the brainstorming.
- The team (or player) who comes up with the most ORIGINAL answers under each category wins the game. To determine originality, groups or players should work together, exchange lists and draw lines through any name that is repeated on both lists. If working in groups, the students should regroup and redo the process until all lists have been compared. In the end the student(s) should count up how many names they have, and the one with the most ORIGINAL names wins. (You may wish to offer a small prize for incentive.)
- Have them share their results, explaining unusual or unknown listings as appropriate.
- Then distribute "By the Book." The student(s) should identify the protagonist, antagonist, and at least one other main character in the novel they are reading to complete the Venn diagram, noting characteristics about each.
- Have them share and compare their ideas and discuss.

Who's Who?

Oliver Twist
By Charles Dickens

In *Oliver Twist* Dickens shows his readers the underbelly of dirty, industrial England in the early 18th century. The story surrounds a poor boy of the title's name and his struggles amidst the poverty of that time. It is an excellent story with many interesting characters, including four that are arguably most important to the tale.

The infant, given the name Oliver Twist, is born to a dying woman in a workhouse. After a terrible early childhood in a baby farm, Oliver is sent to work at the age of nine and treated even worse. After an unjust beating, he escapes and goes to London where, hungry and tired, he falls under the influence of the evil Fagin and his gang of pickpockets.

The criminals hold Oliver captive, teaching him the tricks and trade of street crime. During this period he befriends one of the gang members called the Artful Dodger, who manages to bring Oliver into several brushes with the law. Despite the trouble he causes Oliver, the Artful Dodger also helps in a number of ways as well.

At one point Oliver does manage to escape the streets with the aid of Mr. Brownlow. Mr. Brownlow believes in Oliver's goodness, takes him in, and cares for him when no one else will. But when Oliver is recaptured by Fagin and forced back on the streets, he must once more prove he is worthy of kindness.

In the end with Mr. Brownlow's guidance, Oliver is able to turn his life around. All eventually works out well for him, and he is adopted by the kindhearted man.

Novels usually include many important characters. Read the definitions of the different character types and tell which person in Dickens' novel fits each role and why.

The **protagonist** is the main character in a story.

The **antagonist** is the character who represents the obstacles the protagonist must overcome.

The **foil** is often a sidekick or companion to the protagonist that may contrast the personality of the protagonist in order to highlight his/her strengths and weaknesses.

The **mentor** is a good character that helps the protagonist, often bringing out key values and a sense of purpose.

©InspirEd Educators, Inc.

Fill 'Em Up!

DIRECTIONS: Fill in as many examples of each character role as you can think of from books, movies, and television before time is called.

PROTAGONISTS	ANTAGONISTS	FOILS

MENTORS

BY THE BOOK

DIRECTIONS: Use the triple Venn diagram to compare and contrast the protagonist, antagonist, and other characters in your book.

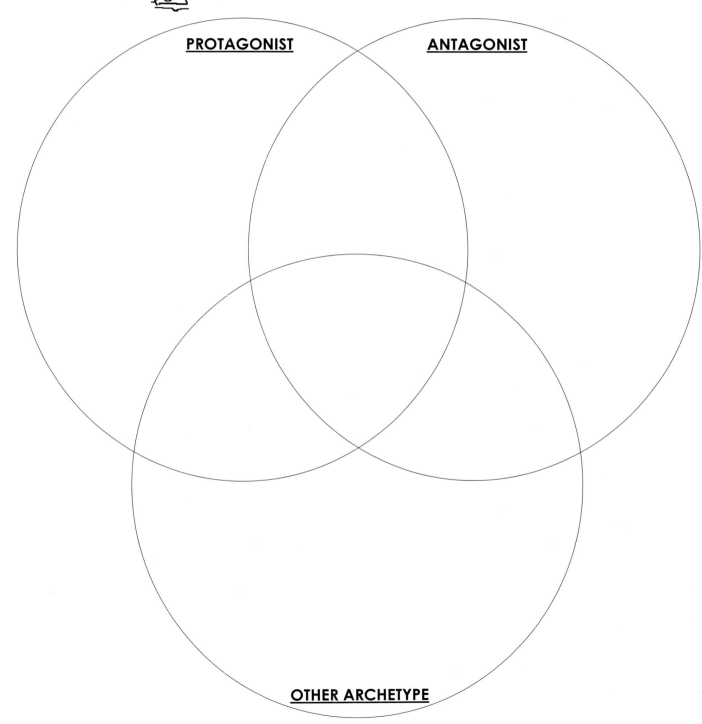

©InspirEd Educators, Inc.

From the Horse's Mouth

Springboard:
Students should complete "Quotable Notables.".
(Answers may vary, but should reflect an understanding that what people and characters say can provide important clues about them.)

Objective: The student will be able to describe how dialogue helps authors make characters come to life.

Materials: Quotable Notables (Springboard handout)
When Scarlett O'Hara Speaks ... (handout)
"Quoting" Characters (handout)

Terms to Know: **dialogue** - speech in a piece of writing shown in quotes

Procedure:
- After reviewing the Springboard, explain that _we can learn a lot about a person or, in the case of literature, a character based on what they say_. Go on to explain that _this lesson examines how authors use dialogue in developing their characters_.
- Distribute "When Scarlett O'Hara Speaks" and review the directions. The student(s) should work independently or in pairs to read the excerpts from Gone with the Wind and write a short character description.
- Have student(s) discuss their paragraphs and discuss how Margaret Mitchell, the author of Gone with the Wind, made use of dialogue to develop her character of Scarlett O'Hara.
- Then distribute "'Quoting' Characters." The student(s) should use the novel they are reading to identify important quotes and analyze how and why each was used to develop the characters. *(Answers will of course vary based on the book, but they should make sense and spark discussion.)*
- Have the student(s) share and compare their quotes and discuss.

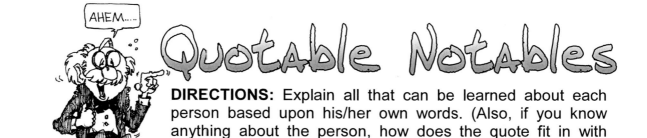

Quotable Notables

DIRECTIONS: Explain all that can be learned about each person based upon his/her own words. (Also, if you know anything about the person, how does the quote fit in with what you know?)

"An eye for eye only ends up making the whole world blind." (Mahatma Gandhi)

"If you can't feed a hundred people, then feed just one." (Mother Teresa)

"The important thing is not to stop questioning. Curiosity has its own reason for existing." (Albert Einstein)

"Darkness cannot drive out darkness; only light can do that. Hate cannot drive out hate; only love can do that." (Dr. Martin Luther King, Jr.)

"Democracy is worth dying for, because it's the most deeply honorable form of government ever devised by man." (President Ronald Reagan)

Based on this activity, why do you think authors often use dialogue in novels?

_____
_____
_____
_____
_____
_____

©InspirEd Educators, Inc.

35

When Scarlett O'Hara Speaks...

DIRECTIONS: Study the quotes from Scarlett O'Hara in <u>Gone with the Wind</u> and write a paragraph to describe the character.

"Great balls of fire! Don't bother me anymore, and don't call me sugar."

"I can't think about that right now. If I do, I'll go crazy. I'll think about that tomorrow."

"I never heard of such bad taste."

"I can shoot straight, if I don't have to shoot too far."

"No! I'm going to have a good time today... And do my eating at the barbeque."

"Great balls of fire! (HICCUP!) It's Rhett!"

"Marriage, fun? Fiddle-dee-dee. Fun for men you mean."

"You'd rather live with that silly little fool who can't open her mouth except to say "yes" or "no" and raise a passel of mealy-mouthed brats just like her."

"If I said I was madly in love with you you'd know I was lying."

"Ooh, if I just wasn't a lady, WHAT wouldn't I tell that varmint!"

"As God is my witness, they're not going to lick me. I'm going to live through this and when it's all over, I'll never be hungry again. No, nor any of my folk. If I have to lie, steal, cheat or kill. As God is my witness, I'll never be hungry again!"

_____

_____

_____

_____

_____

_____

_____

_____

_____

_____

_____

©InspirEd Educators, Inc.

"Quoting" Characters

DIRECTIONS: Complete the graphic organizer using quotes and other information from the novel you are reading. Request additional organizers as needed.

Character:	Quotes:	Why you think the author used each:

Character:	Quotes:	Why you think the author used each:

Character:	Quotes:	Why you think the author used each:

Character:	Quotes:	Why you think the author used each:

©InspirEd Educators, Inc.

Tellers of Tales

Springboard:
Students should complete "The Camping Trip."

Objective: The student will be able to explain how point of view can change the feel of a story.

Materials:	The Camping Trip (Springboard handout)
	The Outsiders (handout)
	The Power of Change (handout)

Terms to know: **narrator** - story teller
first person - story told by a person in the story
third person - story told by someone who is not involved in the story, an outside observer who may or may not be able to tell what characters are thinking

Procedure:
- After reviewing the Springboard, explain that *in this lesson the student(s) will learn how the "voice" of a story can change the way it feels to the reader.*
- Review the terms and then distribute "The Outsiders." Have the student(s) read and complete the handout individually or in pairs.
- Have the student(s) share and compare their ideas. (*The passage is written in the first person, and re-writings may vary.*) Include the following questions in a follow-up discussion:
  - ? How did the story change when told from another point of view? (*Answers will vary, but telling the story from a character's personal point of view may make the story more biased. Also, the reader may feel like he/she knows more about Ponyboy in the first person account.*)
  - ? Why is it important to know who the narrator is in a story? (*Answers may vary but should reflect an understanding that the voice changes the feel of a story. First person accounts often feel more personal than third person and can provide greater insight into the narrator's attitudes, motivations, and feelings.*)
- Distribute "The Power of Change" and have the student(s) select a short passage from the novel they are reading to rewrite in another point of view.
- Have them share their work and explain how the change affected the feel of the passage.

38 ©InspirEd Educators, Inc.

The Camping Trip

1. The guys had been planning the camping trip for weeks. They were all excited about the school year finally ending and were ready to relax and celebrate. They planned to gather at Nick's house and go up to Lawton's Mountain, do some hiking for a couple of hours, and then build an awesome fire to cook over and hang out around at night. When the big day finally arrived, the gang took off to have some fun and eat some good, charred grub.

2. I couldn't believe the guys invited me on their camping trip! I had heard them talking for weeks about it and assumed I wouldn't be invited since they never included me in the conversation. When they finally asked me, I was really excited! I gathered all my camping gear and sleeping bag. My mom and dad told me to call if anything was amiss and I wanted come home. They keep telling me the guys aren't good friends and are mean to me sometimes. Whatever! So when I got to Nick's everyone else was already there. As we drove up to Lawton's Mountain, though, I got a strange feeling that they had been talking about me before I arrived. Sure they invited me; but what would this trip hold in store? I was definitely starting to second-guess my decision to come.

How are the two passages the same? How do they differ? _____

_____

How does the "feel" of the story change from the first passage to the second? _____

_____

_____

Which passage do you think more accurately describes the events? Why? _____

_____

_____

Which story do you think is more interesting to read? Why? _____

_____

_____

What do you think might happen next in the story? _____

_____

_____

©InspirEd Educators, Inc.

The Camping Trip Suggestions for Answers

> 1. The guys had been planning the camping trip for weeks. They were all excited about the school year finally ending and were ready to relax and celebrate. They planned to gather at Nick's house and go up to Lawton's Mountain, do some hiking for a couple of hours, and then build an awesome fire to cook over and hang out around at night. When the big day finally arrived, the gang took off to have some fun and eat some good, charred grub.
>
> 2. I couldn't believe the guys invited me on their camping trip! I had heard them talking for weeks about it and assumed I wouldn't be invited since they never included me in the conversation. When they finally asked me, I was really excited! I gathered all my camping gear and sleeping bag. My mom and dad told me to call if anything was amiss and I wanted come home. They keep telling me the guys aren't good friends and are mean to me sometimes. Whatever! So when I got to Nick's everyone else was already there. As we drove up to Lawton's Mountain, though, I got a strange feeling that they had been talking about me before I arrived. Sure they invited me; but what would this trip hold in store? I was definitely starting to second-guess my decision to come.

How are the two passages the same? How do they differ? *The two passages are alike in that they both are telling about the same event and characters. They both mention some of the same details such as where the event took place, what happened when the guys arrived, etc. The main difference is the narrator; the first passage is told from the view of an observer, and the second by one of the boys going on the camping trip.*

How does the "feel" of the story change in the two passages? *The first story feels like a simple re-telling of a story. It does not include any real emotion but simply states the facts of what happens. The second story includes how a character felt about the events taking place – first he is excited and surprised about being invited, but then seems to hint that something may be amiss.*

Which passage do you think more accurately describes the events? Why? *Answers will vary. Some students may think the first description is accurate because the person telling the story is just reporting the events as a non-biased narrator. Others may think a more accurate depiction of events can be had from someone who is actually involved in the story.*

Which story do you think is more interesting to read? Why? *Answers will vary but should be justified and spark discussion.*

What do you think might happen next in the story? *Answers will vary.*

The OUTSIDERS by S.E. Hinton

Then there were shouts and the pounding of feet, and the Socs jumped up and left me lying there, gasping. I lay there and wondered what in the world was happening -- people were jumping over me and running by me and I was too dazed to figure it out. Then someone had me under the armpits and was hauling me to my feet. It was Darry.

"Are you all right, Ponyboy?"

He was shaking me and I wished he'd stop. I was dizzy enough anyway. I could tell it was Darry though -- partly because of the voice and partly because Darry's always rough with me without meaning to be.

"I'm okay. Quit shaking me, Darry, I'm okay."

He stopped instantly. "I'm sorry."

He wasn't really. Darry isn't ever sorry for anything he does. It seems funny to me that he should look just exactly like my father and act exactly the opposite from him. My father was only forty when he died and he looked twenty-five and a lot of people thought Darry and Dad were brothers instead of father and son. But they only looked alike -- my father was never rough with anyone without meaning to be.

Darry is six-feet-two, and broad-shouldered and muscular. He has dark-brown hair that kicks out in front and a slight cowlick in the back -- just like Dad's -- but Darry's eyes are his own. He's got eyes that are like two pieces of pale blue-green ice. They've got a determined set to them, like the rest of him. He looks older than twenty -- tough, cool, and smart. He would be real handsome if his eyes weren't so cold. He doesn't understand anything that is not plain hard fact. But he uses his head.

I sat down again, rubbing my cheek where I'd been slugged the most.

Darry jammed his fists in his pockets. "They didn't hurt you too bad, did they?"

They did. I was smarting and aching and my chest was sore and I was so nervous my hands were shaking and I wanted to start bawling, but you just don't say that to Darry.

"I'm okay."

Who is the narrator of this novel excerpt? How do you know? _____

_____

_____

Re-write the passage as an outside observer might describe the situation. _____

_____

_____

_____

_____

_____

_____

_____

How does the change in narrator affect the feel of the passage? _____

_____

_____

©InspirEd Educators, Inc.

DIRECTIONS: Select a short passage from the novel you are reading. Identify which point of view it is written in and then re-write it from another point of view. Be prepared to explain how the different point of view might change the story.

Book _____ Page # _____

Original Point of View _____ New Point of View _____

Putting Up a Fight

Springboard:

Students should complete "What Is Conflict?"
(Examples will vary but should illustrate the descriptions given.
Answers to the question will vary but should reflect an understanding
that conflict makes a story more interesting and creates the story action.)

Objective: The student will be able to describe the various types of conflict and explain how it enhances a story.

Materials: What Is Conflict? (Springboard handout)
Conflict Cards (card cut-outs)
Keeping Track of Conflict (handout)

Terms to know: **conflict** - a problem or challenge faced by a character in a story
plot - the main series of events in a story that center around the conflict

Procedure:

· After reviewing the Springboard, explain that *in this lesson the student(s) will examine the role conflict plays in a novel.*

· **For group instruction** organize student(s) into groups of three or four, giving each a "Conflict Card." Have them create a short skit to depict the scenario, adding one of the four types of conflict to the story. **For individual instruction** have the student pick one or more of the scenarios to complete. In order to perform his/her skit, the student can write it as a monologue or use family members or friends to play the parts.

· **NOTE**: If time permits, have the student(s) create multiple skits for each card to exemplify the different types of conflict.

· Have the student(s) perform their skits, having the audience guess what types of conflict are depicted and discuss. During the discussion, make sure the student(s) understand that *the main story, or plot* (review terms), *revolves around conflict, though there are often more than one*. (**NOTE:** Plot is examined in greater detail in subsequent lessons.)

· Distribute "Keeping Track of Conflict" and have the student(s) record what is going on the novel they are reading. **NOTE:** Have the student(s) keep this handout to continue to record what is happening as they finish the book.

©InspirEd Educators, Inc.   43

What Is Conflict?

DIRECTIONS: Conflicts can arise in several ways in literature. For each type of conflict described, think of an example from a book, movie, TV show, etc. and explain it.

Man vs. Man: This type of conflict occurs when one character has a problem or struggle with another character in the story.

Example: _____

_____

_____

_____

Man vs. Society: This type of conflict occurs when a character faces problems or struggles against a government or other larger element of society over which they have no control.

Example: _____

_____

_____

_____

Man vs. Self: This type of conflict occurs when a character struggles with something personal that has nothing to do with other characters in the story.

Example: _____

_____

_____

_____

Man vs. Nature: This type of conflict occurs when a character has to deal with something in nature. It could be a disaster such as a tornado, fire, or flood or common elements such as drought, periods of rain, sweltering heat, etc.

Example: _____

_____

_____

_____

Choose one of your examples and explain why it is important to the story. _____

_____

_____

_____

_____

_____

CONFLICT CARDS

A man is walking his dog.	A woman is going to interview for a new job.
A group of friends are on a camping trip.	A little girl is getting ready for her dance recital.
A young boy is trying out for the school play.	An old woman is going to her weekly bingo game.
A businessman is sitting in traffic on his way home from work.	A teenage boy is buying his first car.
An honor student is preparing for his final exams	A young woman is planning her wedding.
A high school senior is trying to decide where to go to college.	An adolescent boy is going to ask a girl to the school dance.
A family is making plans for their summer vacation.	A newlywed is shopping for a birthday present for her new husband.

©InspirEd Educators, Inc.

Keeping Track of Conflict

DIRECTIONS: Use the organizer to record examples you find of each type of conflict that occurs in your novel. For each, be sure to explain the conflict and how it enhances the story.

Man vs. Man:	Man vs. Society:
Man vs. Self:	Man vs. Nature:

46 ©InspirEd Educators, Inc.

Plotting

> **Springboard:**
> Students should read and complete the "Cinderella" handout.

Objective: Students will be able to trace and explain the elements of plot in a story.

Materials:	Cinderella (Springboard handout) The Plots Thicken (handout) A Story with BIG Holes (handout) Plot Diagram for: (handout)
Terms to know:	**exposition** - the story background and introduction **inciting force** - situation that triggers story conflict **rising action** - events building up to the story's climax **climax** - the high point of the conflict which becomes the turning point of the story **falling action** - events that lead to the solution of the conflict in a story **resolution** - the way the conflict works out (can be positive or negative) **foreshadowing** - clues to future events

Procedure:

- While discussing the Springboard, review the related definitions. *(Answers will of course vary and should be briefly explained.)* Then explain that <u>this lesson examines how authors "build" plots in novels</u>.

- Distribute "The Plots Thicken." Have the student(s) work individually or in pairs to plot two other fairy tales, books, or movies and share their ideas. *(Answers will vary, should be explained and make sense.)*

- Distribute "A Story with BIG Holes." The student(s) should work individually or in pairs to fill in the blanks in the story with people, actions, and events that present the plot elements as noted.

- Then explain that <u>to make stories more interesting and pull the reader in, authors often give hints to events that are yet to occur. Sometimes such hints can lead the reader to predict the events to come, or possibly throw the reader "off the scent" to develop an element of surprise</u>. (Introduce the term "foreshadowing".)

- Then have the student(s) share their stories and, as they do, have others listen and try to find places the author(s) could have inserted foreshadowing to influence the reader's ideas and make the story more interesting.

- Distribute the "Plot Diagram for: ____" handout and have the student(s) begin to fill in the information about their books. They should continue to fill in information as they progress in their reading.

©InspirEd Educators, Inc.

Cinderella

Practically everyone has read or seen *Cinderella*, the story of a beautiful orphaned girl raised by her cruel stepmother. For years she works as a servant for her evil parent and ugly stepsisters, until she is finally pulled from her misery by a handsome prince. This tale easily shows how plot works in a simple story.

DIRECTIONS: Study the plot diagram for *Cinderella* and try to briefly explain or write a definition of your own for each plot-related term below.

CLIMAX: Cinderella attends the ball and spends a wonderful evening with the prince, before she abruptly runs away at midnight.

RISING ACTION: There is much preparation in Cinderella's home, but great disappointment for her. She cannot go to the ball, lacking a gown, having only rags to wear.
Her fairy godmother comes and decks her out, so she can attend; but with a warning that all the magic will disappear at midnight.

FALLING ACTION: Smitten, the prince sets out to find his new love, but his only clue to her identity is the glass slipper she left behind when she fled the night before. Word is sent to everyone in the kingdom that whomever the glass slipper fits will become the prince's bride. Despite all efforts of others including Cinderella's ugly and mean stepsisters, the prince has no luck... UNTIL...

INCITING FORCE: The family learns of a ball to be held to introduce the prince to local young women, in hopes of finding a wife.

EXPOSITION: Cinderella lives a miserable life, slaving away for her cruel stepmother and her two ugly, foolish stepsisters.

RESOLUTION: Cinderella is able to make her way to the prince and try on the slipper, proving herself to be the prince's lost love. The two are then married and live happily ever after.

Exposition - _____

_____

Inciting Force - _____

_____

Rising Action - _____

_____

Climax - _____

_____

Falling Action - _____

_____

Resolution - _____

_____

The Plots Thicken

TITLE:

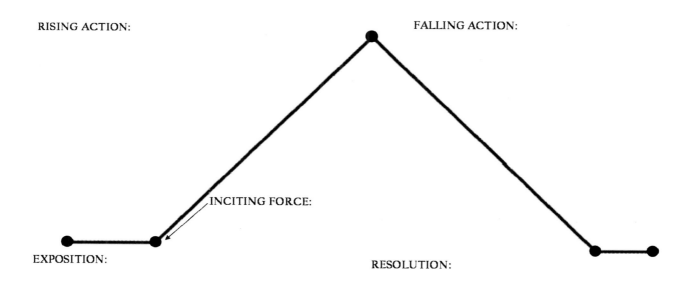

TITLE:

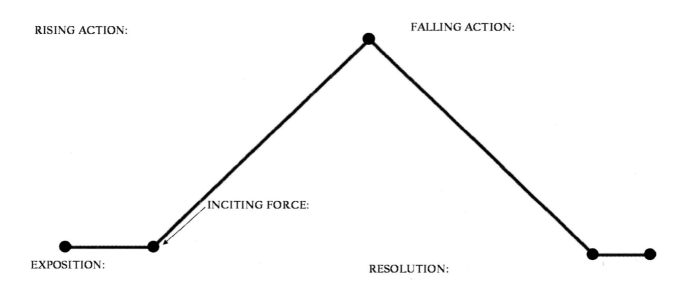

©InspirEd Educators, Inc.

49

A Story with BIG Holes

Once upon a time there was (a, an)_____
who was very _____
_____
_____ (exposition).
Now this (person, animal, _____) was very _____
which was always causing (him, her) all kinds of trouble. There was the
time that _____
_____
_____
(conflict example) and then it happened again, but (better, worse).
    One day _____ was going to _____
_____
_____ (setting up the climax)
when as if from nowhere, _____
_____
_____
_____ (inciting force).
(He, she) was _____
_____ so the only thing there
was to do was to _____
_____
so (he, she) did. It was _____ but (he, she) _____
_____
_____ (climax).
    A few (days, weeks, months, years) later, _____
_____
_____.
No one expected or could have predicted that _____
_____
_____
_____
and before long _____
_____
_____ (falling action).
    While it wasn't what was expected, it was _____
_____
_____
and proved _____
_____
_____ (resolution).

50   ©InspirEd Educators, Inc.

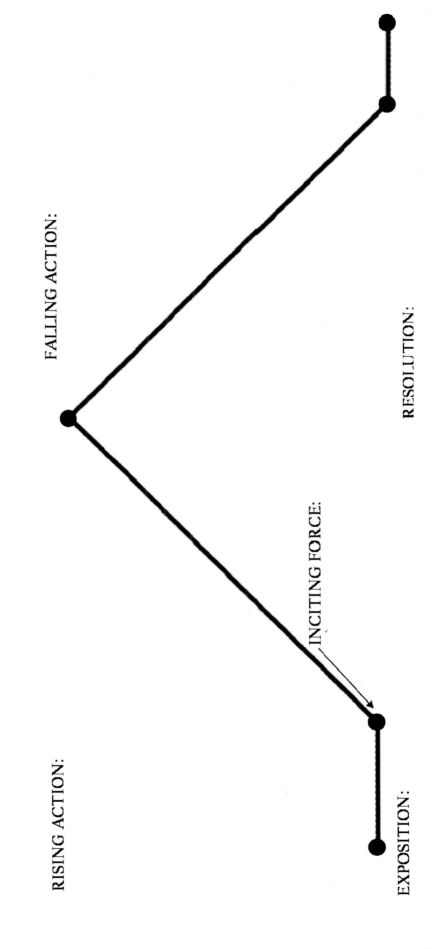

Look Around

Springboard:
The student should read "The Pond" and answer the questions.
(Answers will vary but should be logical based on the reading.)

Objective: The student will be able to explain how setting affects and enhances a story.

Materials:
The Pond (Springboard handout)
Mix & Match (cut-outs)
It's a Set-Up (handout)
Show Me the Setting! (handout)
art supplies

Terms to know:
setting - the surroundings, times, and places where events in a story occur

Procedure:
· While reviewing the Springboard, have the student(s) offer examples of the various elements of setting *(in a forest, at midnight, etc.)*. Explain that _in addition to characters and plot, the setting is also usually a very important element of the story. Time and place, sights and sounds DO matter!_

· Distribute the "Mix and Match" and "It's a Set-Up" handouts. The student(s) should work individually, in pairs, or small groups to cut out the cards and create three groups that "fit" together, including as many words as they can. They should then use their groupings to complete "It's a Set-Up" as directed.

· Have the student(s) share their writings and discuss how the various settings might fit into a complete story.

· **EXTENSION:** The student(s) could choose one of their setting descriptions to complete a plot diagram and/or write a story that takes place there.

· Distribute "Show Me the Setting!" Review the instructions and give the student(s) time to brainstorm their ideas. Then, depending on how much time you want to devote, either have the student(s) complete their visual representations in class or at home.

· Have them share their ideas and discuss how the setting enhances (or should enhance) the novel they are reading *(If well-written, it should provide the reader with a vivid picture of where the story takes place and the conditions under which the action occurs.)*

"The pond Sam had discovered on that spring morning was seldom visited by any human being. All winter, snow had covered the ice; the pond lay cold and still under its white blanket. Most of the time there wasn't a sound to be heard. The frog was asleep. Occasionally a jay would cry out. And sometimes at night the fox would bark – a high, rasping bark. Winter seemed to last forever.

But one day a change came over the woods and the pond. Warm air, soft and kind, blew through the trees. The ice, which had softened during the night, began to melt. Patches of open water appeared. All the creatures that lived in the pond and in the woods were glad to feel the warmth. They heard and felt the breath of spring, and they stirred with new life and hope. There was a good, new smell in the air, a smell of earth waking after its long sleep. The frog, buried in the mud at the bottom of the pond, knew that spring was here. The chickadee knew and was delighted (almost everything delights a chickadee). The vixen, dozing in her den, knew she would soon have kits. Every creature knew that a better, easier time was at hand – warmer days, pleasanter nights. Trees were putting out green buds; the buds were swelling. Birds began arriving from the south. A pair of ducks flew in. The Red-winged Blackbird arrived and scouted the pond for nesting sites. A small sparrow with a white throat arrived and sang, "Oh, sweet Canada, Canada, Canada!"

And if you had been sitting by the pond on that first warm day of spring, suddenly, toward the end of the afternoon, you would have heard a stirring sound high above you in the air – a sound like the sound of trumpets."

Excerpt from The Trumpet of the Swan by E.B. White

Describe as many aspects of the setting E.B. White describes as you can. (These can include time, place, season, sights, sounds, etc.) _____
_____
_____
_____
_____
_____

What would it "feel" like to be present in the story? _____
_____
_____
_____

How would the "feeling" change if one of these elements were different? Give at least one example. _____
_____
_____
_____
_____

©InspirEd Educators, Inc.

sunny	stormy	piercing screams	sunset	midnight
muggy	dark	exciting	city	rock 'n roll
chirping	beach	bone-chilling	mountainous	chilled
creepy	exhilarating	deep	rain forest	apartment
mansion	tense	high	grassy	flowers blooming
summer	mild	dripping	starlit	squeaking
crunching	soft	first frost	corn field	farm
new house	dewy	winter	cucumbers	old-fashioned
bouquets	pitch black	cave	howling	bare trees
noon	dreary	slum	wilting flowers	misshapen
ice	spring	soft music	modern	falling leaves
sweltering	smooth	heavy beat	plush grass	high-style
crisp	squawking	hushed tones	office building	mid-afternoon
forest	barn	dawn	shining	autumn

54 ©InspirEd Educators, Inc.

It's a Set-Up

DIRECTIONS: List the three groupings of words you identify. Then, in the blank write what the setting is and then in the space provided, a plot that would "fit" in that setting.

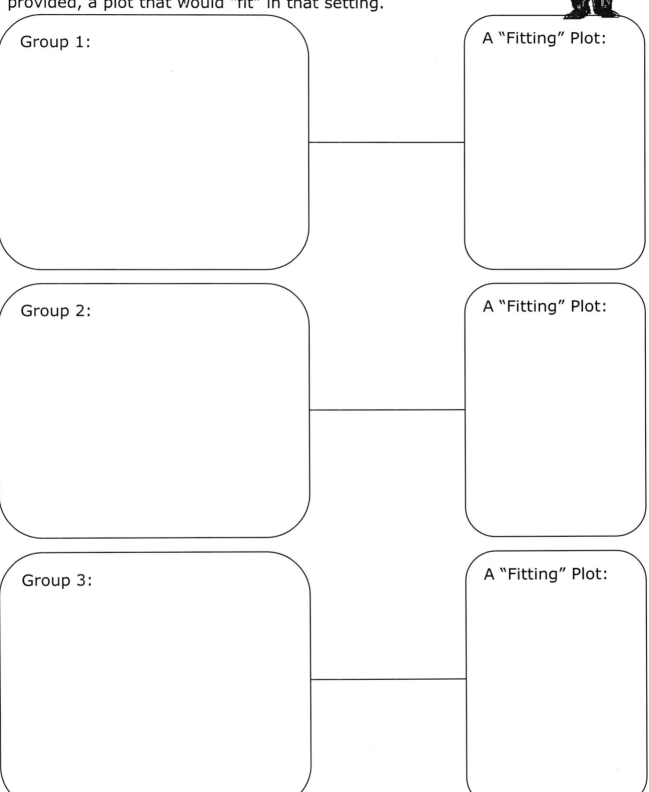

Group 1:

A "Fitting" Plot:

Group 2:

A "Fitting" Plot:

Group 3:

A "Fitting" Plot:

©InspirEd Educators, Inc.

Show Me The Setting!

For this assignment you will create a visual representation of an important setting in the novel you are reading. First, record the elements of the setting in the chart below. Then brainstorm ideas of how you can portray it to others. Some possibilities include:

· a three dimensional model or diorama.
· a collage.
· a brochure.
· a painting or drawing.

Whichever format you choose, make sure you:

· include all five elements of setting from your story.
· create a good "feel" for what it would be like to be in that setting.
· be neat and creative!

Elements of Setting:	Ideas to portray each element:
Time period:	
Location:	
Weather:	
Social Conditions:	
Mood:	

Setting Scoring Guide

Use the following scale to evaluate your work:

4 – excellent   3 – good   2 – fair   1 – poor   0 – unacceptable

	Student Evaluation	Teacher Evaluation
Included all elements	_____	_____
Created a "feel"	_____	_____
Used appropriate format	_____	_____
Neat and creative	_____	_____

Grade:

Comments:

56   ©InspirEd Educators, Inc.

The Power of Words

Springboard: Students should read the excepts and complete "What's the Difference? *(Answers will vary but should make sense.)*

Objective: The student will be able to explain how imagery helps to develop setting.

Materials: What's the Difference? (Springboard handout)
Trading Places (handout)
Can Ya' See It? Do Ya' Feel It? (handout)

Terms to know: **imagery** - use of words to create sensory experiences
sensory - having to do with sight, sound, taste, touch, and smell

Procedure:
- As the student(s) share answers to the Springboard, explain that <u>authors use descriptive wording to make their setting more real</u>. Then discuss the following questions:
    - ? How are the student descriptions different from the originals? Give examples. *(In each case the original used more description language; specific examples may vary.)*
    - ? (If not pointed out, introduce the terms "imagery" and "sensory.") What words do the authors use to make the reader see, hear, feel, taste, or smell? *(Answers may vary but should make sense.)*
- Distribute the "Trading Places" handout and explain that in this activity the student(s) will be the authors. Have the student(s) work individually or in pairs to complete the activity.
- Have them share / compare their descriptions and the different sensory experiences they provide.
- Then distribute the "Can Ya' See It? Do Ya' Feel It?" handout and have the student(s) evaluate the setting description in the novel they're reading.

©InspirEd Educators, Inc.

WHAT'S THE DIFFERENCE?

DIRECTIONS: Read each setting description and write your own, simpler description of the scene.

"Dicey looked out the window and made her legs stay still. Outside, wind blew the branches of the two big oaks, ripping off the last of the brown leaves and carrying them away. The sky was a bright blue, and the sun shone with a diamond hardness. The brightness of the sun and the coldness of the wind combined to mark out sharply the edges of her view. She could see each individual rock on the old building, as if the cold made each brick contract into itself. The angles of the main entranceway, the clear edge of the cement sidewalk, the flat lawn, bare and brown now, all looked as if they would be cold to the touch."

Excerpt from Dicey's Song by Cynthia Voigt

_____

_____

_____

_____

"Maycomb was an old town, but it was a tired old town ... In rainy weather the streets turned to red slop; grass grew on the sidewalks, the courthouse sagged in the square. Somehow, it was hotter then: a black dog suffered on a summers day; bony mules hitched to Hoover carts flicked flies in the sweltering shade of the live oaks on the square. Men's stiff collars wilted by nine in the morning. Ladies bathed before noon, after their tree-o'clock naps, and by nightfall were like soft teacakes with frostings of sweat and sweet talcum."

Excerpt from To Kill a Mockingbird by Harper Lee

_____

_____

_____

_____

"He could not see the green of the shore now but only the tops of the blue hills that showed white as though they were snow-capped and the clouds that looked like high mountains above them. The sea was very dark and the light made prisms in the water." *Excerpt from The Old Man and the Sea by Ernest Hemingway*

_____

_____

_____

_____

DIRECTIONS: Read each setting description and then write your own, adding descriptive language and other details to help the reader see, feel, etc. the scene.

It was a cold November morning. A light drizzle fell splattering on the puddles that formed from yesterday's rains. Water dripped from awnings all along Main Street.

___

It's springtime in the country. The sky is blue, the flowers are blooming, and the birds are rushing around building nests.

___

©InspirEd Educators, Inc.

Can Ya' See It? Do Ya' Feel It?

DIRECTIONS: Find two setting descriptions and provide the information shown. Then mark an "X" on each line below to tell how clear of a sensory experience it provides and explain why below.

Description (and page #) - _____
_____
_____
_____
_____

Importance to story - _____
_____
_____
_____

NOT   ⟵━━━━━━━━━━━━━━━━━━⟶   **VERY**
Vivid   Vivid

Description (and page #) - _____
_____
_____
_____
_____

Importance to story - _____
_____
_____
_____

NOT   ⟵━━━━━━━━━━━━━━━━━━⟶   **VERY**
Vivid   Vivid

A Way with Words

Springboard:
> Students should study the lists and complete the "Fitting the Mold" handout as directed.

Objective: Students explain different ways authors use figurative language to enhance the story.

Materials:
Fitting the Mold (Springboard handout)
Memory Boosters (handout)
What Is the Use? (handout)

Terms to know:
alliteration - two or more words with the same beginning consonant sound grouped for effect
assonance - two or more words with the same sounds within them
simile - figure of speech where two unlike things are compared using "as" or "like"
metaphor - figure of speech describing something in terms of another without using "as" or "like"
idiom - a common expression that has no connection to the literal meaning of the words
onomatopoeia - words that imitate sounds

Procedure:
- (**NOTE:** The Springboard may take a little longer than usual to complete.) During discussion of the Springboard, introduce and define each of the "Terms to know," listed in order (left to right in rows) as the lists appear. Then as the student(s) share their added examples, have others guess which literary term applies to each.
- Distribute the "Memory Boosters" handout and explain that _the various types of figurative language in this lesson can be confusing and hard to remember_. Go on to explain that _in this lesson the student(s) will try to come up with ways to keep them straight_. The student(s) should work individually or in groups (if at all possible) to think of memory strategies to distinguish the different types of figurative language.
- Have them share their ideas and discuss. *(Answers may vary, but the process of figuring out how to remember and distinguish the terms should help for future reference.)*
- Distribute the "What Is the Use?" page and review the directions. The student(s) should then work individually or in small groups, examining their own novel and others to find at least one example of each type of figurative language (but the more the better).
- Have them share what they find and discuss including the following questions:
  - ? Why would authors use figurative language? *(To make a story more real, vivid, literary; to add humor, etc.)*
  - ? When might an author not want to use such devices? *(In some dialogue it may sound odd; in serious situations onomatopoeia may not work, etc.)*

©InspirEd Educators, Inc.
61

"Fitting the Mold"

DIRECTIONS: Note what you think each list of phrases has in common, and write your answer on the line. (If you can actually name the category, it's a bonus!) Then try to add one or two more examples to each list

_____

bugs black blood
wild and wooly, walrus
Wild, Wild West
sea shells at the sea shore
man-made matters
safe and sound
sweet smell of success
magnificent mountains
big, brown bear

_____

_____

_____

No way, José!
wet head in bed
six sick kids
sticky wicket
home grown ghost
light my fire
geek week at Peak Street
May's saving grace
The Mad Hatter

_____

_____

_____

white as a sheet
blind as a bat
eat like a horse
face like an angel
sick as a dog
walk like an Egyptian
closed up like a clam
mad as a hornet
swim like a fish

_____

_____

_____

Dad exploded!
hair of golden silk
steel wool hair
eat a horse
the world is a stage
bridge to the past
whispering raindrops
sea of grass
ghostly shadows

_____

_____

_____

long road to hoe
the early bird
adding fuel to the fire
raining cats and dogs
costs an arm and a leg
footing the bill
in a pickle
kick the bucket
snake in the grass

_____

_____

_____

Crash! Bang!
GRRRRR!
clip-clop, clip-clop
ring, ring
bzzzzzzzzzz
squeak, squeak
caw, caw, caw
knock-knock
vroom-vroom

_____

_____

? Why do you think authors might want to use these kinds of phrases in their writings? _____

_____

_____

_____

62   ©InspirEd Educators, Inc.

MEMORY BOOSTERS

DIRECTIONS: Brainstorm ways to help you and others remember which examples of figurative language are which.

Alliteration	Assonance	Simile
Metaphor	Idiom	Onomatopoeia

©InspirEd Educators, Inc.

63

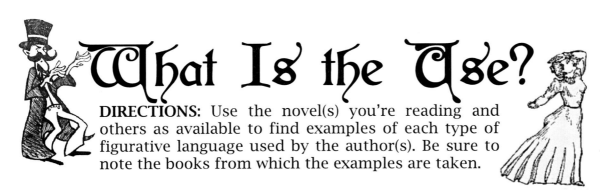

What Is the Use?

DIRECTIONS: Use the novel(s) you're reading and others as available to find examples of each type of figurative language used by the author(s). Be sure to note the books from which the examples are taken.

Alliteration: _____

Assonance: _____

Simile: _____

Metaphor: _____

Idiom: _____

Onomatopoeia: _____

©InspirEd Educators, Inc.

In a Good Mood?

Springboard:
Students should read "Getting 'Real'" and answer the questions.
(Many sensory descriptions; figurative language: "hard as concrete" is a simile, "he roared" and the "water trying to kill him" are metaphors; crashing, ripping, and slam are onomatopoeia. The mood is of confusion and terror. Use of clear, sensory descriptions and use of figurative language help develop the "feel.")

Objective: The student will be able to identify the "mood" of a written piece and the wording that helps create it.

Materials:
Getting "Real" (Springboard handout)
Moody Words (handout)
Create Two Moods (handout)

Terms to know:
mood - the "feeling" the author creates for the reader

Procedure:

- During discussion of the Springboard, introduce the term "mood" and have the student(s) tell what the mood of the passage is. *(It's the same as the "feeling" the readers get.)* Explain that <u>in this lesson the student(s) will experiment with mood and descriptive language</u>.

- Distribute the "Moody Words" handout. The student(s) should work individually, in pairs, or groups to study each picture and brainstorm words and phrases that contribute to the perceived mood.

- Have them share / compare answers and discuss. *(Answers will vary, but note particularly colorful, sensory, and figurative language.)*

- Then hand out the "Create Two Moods" page and have the student(s) write two paragraphs developing one of the moods from the previous handout or any others of choice.

- Again have them share paragraphs, pointing out particularly effective groupings of words and phrases (and **for group instruction** having others guess the mood and point out effective wording) and explaining each.

©InspirEd Educators, Inc.   65

Getting "Real"

"There was a great wrenching as the wings caught the pines at the side of the clearing and broke back, ripping back just outside the main braces... Then a wild crashing sound, ripping of metal and the plane rolled to the right and blew through the trees, out over the water and down, down to slam into the lake, skip once on water as hard as concrete, water that tore the windshield out and shattered the side windows, water that drove him back into the seat. Somebody was screaming, screaming as the plane drove down into the water. Someone screamed tight animal screams of fear and pain and he did not know that it was his sound, that he roared against the water that took him and the plane still deeper, down in the water. He saw nothing but sensed the blue, cold blue-green, and he raked at the seatbelt catch, tore his nails loose on one hand. He ripped at it until it released and somehow – the water trying to kill him, to end him – somehow he pulled himself out of the shattered front window and clawed up into the blue, felt something hold him back, felt his windbreaker tear and he was free. Tearing free. Ripping free."

Excerpt from <u>Hatchet</u> by Gary Paulsen

What words provide a "sensory" description of the scene? _____

_____

_____

_____

_____

What examples of figurative language did the author use in this short passage? Be specific as to the kinds. _____

_____

_____

_____

What "feelings" did the author help the reader experience in this scene?

_____

_____

_____

_____

How can an author help the reader experience what is happening in a novel? _____

_____

_____

_____

MOODY Words

DIRECTIONS: List words and phrases that would help develop the "mood" of each picture in the space provided at the side.

©InspirEd Educators, Inc.

67

Create Two Moods

DIRECTIONS: Decide upon two "moods" such as excitement, anger, fear, giddiness, warmth, cold and uninviting, etc. and write a paragraph describing scenes to create each mood. Be sure to use sensory descriptions and, if possible, some figurative language as well.

MOOD: _____

_____
_____
_____
_____
_____
_____
_____
_____
_____
_____
_____
_____

MOOD: _____

_____
_____
_____
_____
_____
_____
_____
_____
_____
_____
_____
_____

©InspirEd Educators, Inc.

It Is What It Is, Or Is It?

Springboard: Students should read "Speaking of Symbols" and answer the questions.

Objective: The student will be able to identify and explain symbolism in a novel or other literary work.

Materials: Speaking of Symbols (Springboard handout)
What Is the Meaning of This?! (handout)
Going by the Book (handout)

Terms to know: **symbol** - a person, place, or thing in a story that represents something other than itself
context - circumstances or placement of use

Procedure:
- After reviewing the Springboard, explain that *in this lesson the student(s) will consider the importance of props and objects to characters in a story*.
- Distribute "What Is the Meaning of This?!" The student(s) should work individually, in pairs, or small groups to complete the handout as directed.
- Have the student(s) share / compare their ideas and discuss. (*Answers may vary, but the examples should make sense and support the meaning.*) During the discussion, have the student(s) explain why answers can differ for an assignment like this. (*The symbolism differs according to its usage. For example the clock, which would mean time to most people, could represent the passage of time during a meeting or years if it moves quickly. It could also symbolize being late or early, morning or night, a mealtime, etc. depending upon context.*)
- Distribute "Going by the Book" and review the directions. The student(s) should then work individually (with assistance as needed) to find three symbols in the novel they're reading, and explain each as directed. (**NOTE:** This can also be a long-term assignment, if desired.)
- Have them share their symbol ideas and discuss.

©InspirEd Educators, Inc.

#*% $ρΣ@ķ!Ŋġ ΩF δψШβΘ£ς &=$

A symbol can be a person, place, or object; what makes it symbolic is that it stands for something greater than itself. Symbols are common in our world, people use symbols all the time, many of which have the same meaning for everyone. People driving on city streets all know what the traffic lights mean, and when families fly the flag outside their home, anyone seeing it would assume those inside are patriotic. Even words themselves are symbols for whatever they represent: trees; dogs; houses; cars; computers; and so forth.

Yet even symbols that have common meanings can be viewed differently depending upon the situation. For example, a nation's flag may have greater importance to an army veteran than a child pledging allegiance in a first grade class. On the other hand, were a terrorist to see that same flag, it would be viewed as something truly **despicable**. Likewise a millionaire may look at a dollar bill and see it as worthless, while a homeless person might view that same bill as a meal.

Authors often make use of symbols in their writing. At times the symbols may be obvious: a diamond engagement ring and a single red rose at a dinner setting both speak of love. A bloody knife and a room in disarray imply a crime, probably murder. Yet other symbolism is not always as clear and may even mean different things at different times. A candle, for example, may symbolize hope in the darkness or when it burns out, death.

Of course, not every object, place, or person in a story symbolizes something else. More often than not, in fact, a rose is just a rose, or an ocean wave is just that. Still, many literary symbols can be found in novels. However the reader should take care to examine such symbols in the context in which they are used to figure out the author's meaning.

Based on the reading, which of the following do you think would **MOST LIKELY** be used as a symbol in a novel? Explain your reasoning in the space at the right.
    A. a warship
    B. an eggplant
    C. a kitchen table
    D. an ancient scroll

According to the passage, a ___ could mean ___.
    A. symbol … nothing at all
    B. lightbulb … light or an idea
    C. novel … author or reader
    D. racetrack … horses or cows

Which word is a synonym for "despicable" in the second paragraph?
    A. adorable   C. patriotic
    B. probable   D. hateful

When a nurse speaks to a young injured soldier, she **MOST LIKELY** represents
    A. a mother figure.   C. early death.
    B. the cruelty of war.   D. home.

#*% $pΣ@ḳ!Ŋġ ΩF δψⱰβΘ₤ς Answers & Explanations &=$

A symbol can be a person, place, or object; what makes it symbolic is that it stands for something greater than itself. Symbols are common in our world, people use symbols all the time, many of which have the same meaning for everyone. People driving on city streets all know what the traffic lights mean, and when families fly the flag outside their home, anyone seeing it would assume those inside are patriotic. Even words themselves are symbols for whatever they represent: trees; dogs; houses; cars; computers; and so forth.

Yet even symbols that have common meanings can be viewed differently depending upon the situation. For example, a nation's flag may have greater importance to an army veteran than a child pledging allegiance in a first grade class. On the other hand, were a terrorist to see that same flag, it would be viewed as something truly **despicable**. Likewise a millionaire may look at a dollar bill and see it as worthless, while a homeless person might view that same bill as a meal.

Authors often make use of symbols in their writing. At times the symbols may be obvious: a diamond engagement ring and a single red rose at a dinner setting both speak of love. A bloody knife and a room in disarray imply a crime, probably murder. Yet other symbolism is not always as clear and may even mean different things at different times. A candle, for example, may symbolize hope in the darkness or when it burns out, death.

Of course, not every object, place, or person in a story symbolizes something else. More often than not, in fact, a rose is just a rose, or an ocean wave is just that. Still, many literary symbols can be found in novels. However the reader should take care to examine such symbols in the context in which they are used to figure out the author's meaning.

Based on the reading, which of the following do you think would **MOST LIKELY** be used as a symbol in a novel? Explain your reasoning in the space at the right.
    A. a warship
    B. an eggplant   *(Answers may vary. Anything can be used as a symbol*
    C. a kitchen table   *and must be examined in the context of the story to*
    D. an ancient scroll   *determine the meaning.)*

According to the passage, a ___ could mean ___.   *(The answer must fit both blanks*
    A. symbol ... nothing at all   *and make sense. A is incorrect by*
    B. lightbulb ... light or an idea *   *definition; if something in a story has no*
    C. novel ... author or reader   *meaning beyond itself, it isn't a symbol.*
    D. racetrack ... horses or cows   *Choices C and D don't make sense.)*

Which word is a synonym for "despicable" in the second paragraph?
    A. adorable   C. patriotic
    B. probable   D. hateful *
    (A synonym should be able to replace the word in the passage. Choices A-C are generally positive, which is not how a terrorist would view an enemy flag.)

When a nurse speaks to a young injured soldier, she **MOST LIKELY** represents
    A. a mother figure. *   C. early death.
    B. the cruelty of war.   D. home.
    (Though there are many possible meanings for the nurse, of the choices given the mother figure is the best possiblity. However, D could be correct if justified.)

©InspirEd Educators, Inc.

WHat iS tHe Meaning of THiS?!

DIRECTIONS: For each symbol, tell what you think it represents and write a short explanation of how the symbol might be used in a story. Then make up one symbol example of your own.

Symbol	Meaning	Example
clock		
framed picture		
crow		
rifle		
cloak		
apple		
_____		

©InspirEd Educators, Inc.

Going by the Book

DIRECTIONS: Identify three symbols: objects, people (usually not the main characters), or places you think the author meant to have meaning beyond themselves. Explain the context and what you view as the meaning of each.

SYMBOL # 1: _____

Context:

Meaning:

SYMBOL # 2: _____

Context:

Meaning:

SYMBOL # 3: _____

Context:

Meaning:

©InspirEd Educators, Inc.

Get the Message?

Springboard:
   Students should read "What Lies Beneath" and answer the questions.

Objective: The student will be able to explain what themes are and be able to identify them in some literature.

Materials: What Lies Beneath (Springboard handouts)
                        Theme Thinking (handout)

Terms to know: **theme** - a broad idea, meaning, or point of a novel or other work of literature or art
                        improvisation - to invent or compose with little preparation

Procedure:

• During discussion of the Springboard, have the student(s) generate ideas for plots that might have the messages of the last question. *(A character that without faith in himself/herself learns that with effort and persistence, anything is possible. A character has a lengthy and difficult task and procrastinates to avoid it, but learns the best way to finish is to start. A character travels far and wide seeking his/her place, fortune, etc., but learns the best place is home.)*

• Distribute the "Theme Thinking" handout. Have the student(s) work individually or in groups for five minutes or so to brainstorm ideas for how each theme could play out in a story.

• Then introduce the term "improvisation" and explain that <u>the student(s) will be doing some improvisational skits about the themes they considered</u>. **For group instruction** have the students work in small groups, assigning each one of the themes. Allow the groups a few minutes (no more than about five) to discuss ideas for their improvisations. These "stories" need not be detailed; bare bones tales are sufficient. Once they have planned their skits, have each group perform, discussing why and how each skit addresses the assigned theme thereafter. **For individualized instruction** have the student tell short stories for a few of the themes, discussing why and how each story addresses its theme.

• During the follow-up discussion, have the student(s) try to identify the themes in these common tales *(Suggested answers are provided but others are acceptable if logical and well-reasoned, since themes require interpretation)*:
   ○ Little Red Riding Hood - *(Things are not always what they seem; danger sometimes lurks in the familiar; etc.*
   ○ Snow White – *(Goodness prevails over evil; the pure of heart will find their heart's desire; love triumphs over all; etc.)*
   ○ Rumpelstiltskin – *(Lying begets more lying and creates a tangled web; overconfidence can backfire; it never works to pretend to be something, someone, or have some skills you don't; etc.)*

74   ©InspirEd Educators, Inc.

WHAT LIES BENEATH

Most novels or other works of literature and art have a theme, an underlying meaning or a point the author is making. The author may state the theme in the words or actions of a character, or it may be unstated, left for the reader to decide. Unlike the subject or topic, the theme examines something deeper. The subject of a novel is what the author has chosen to write about; the theme would be a view of the subject. For example, a novel might be written about -- the subject or topic – love, while the theme might be that love conquers all.

Themes can be major or minor. A major theme would be one an author and others bring up frequently. They can be lessons learned or situations that are often repeated in art or literature. Minor themes are ideas that may appear from time to time. Themes may be presented in several ways:

- Authors can allow the reader to share the thoughts and feelings of the main character, experiencing and learning what he/she does. A character such as Alice in <u>Alice in Wonderland</u> by Lewis Carroll takes a great journey and has many unusual experiences.
- Authors may use dialogue to bring the reader "inside the mind" of one or more characters. Themes often show up as thoughts the main character has over and over. Dorothy from <u>The Wizard of Oz</u> certainly learned that "home" was the only place she really wanted to be.
- The main character usually illustrates the main theme of the story. Often the theme is what the main character does or learns in the story. Examples include a dangerous or emotional trip, a tremendous sacrifice, learning the value of love or friendship, or discovering some important truth.
- Characters can express the theme through their actions. The characters' actions show the reader what's really important. Winning a great battle, falling from grace for one's misdeeds, solving a mystery, or learning that revenge achieves little but harm.

The theme of a novel could **BEST** be described as
- A. its subject.
- B. the author.
- C. the point.
- D. a thought.

While ___ is the topic of a novel, the theme might be ___.
- A. war … it is useless
- B. man … his thoughts
- C. lessons … learning
- D. home … is a building

Which saying is **LEAST** likely to be the theme of a novel?
- A. Whatever you can conceive and believe, you can achieve.
- B. The journey of a thousand miles begins with a single step.
- C. Home is where the heart is.
- D. A stitch in time saves nine.

©InspirEd Educators, Inc.

WHAT LIES BENEATH
ANSWERS & EXPLANATIONS

Most novels or other works of literature and art have a theme, an underlying meaning or a point the author is making. The author may state the theme in the words or actions of a character, or it may be unstated, left for the reader to decide. Unlike the subject or topic, the theme examines something deeper. The subject of a novel is what the author has chosen to write about; the theme would be a view of the subject. For example, a novel might be written about -- the subject or topic – love, while the theme might be that love conquers all.

Themes can be major or minor. A major theme would be one an author and others bring up frequently. They can be lessons learned or situations that are often repeated in art or literature. Minor themes are ideas that may appear from time to time. Themes may be presented in several ways:

- Authors can allow the reader to share the thoughts and feelings of the main character, experiencing and learning what he/she does. A character such as Alice in <u>Alice in Wonderland</u> by Lewis Carroll takes a great journey and has many unusual experiences.
- Authors may use dialogue to bring the reader "inside the mind" of one or more characters. Themes often show up as thoughts the main character has over and over. Dorothy from <u>The Wizard of Oz</u> certainly learned that "home" was the only place she really wanted to be.
- The main character usually illustrates the main theme of the story. Often the theme is what the main character does or learns in the story. Examples include a dangerous or emotional trip, a tremendous sacrifice, learning the value of love or friendship, or discovering some important truth.
- Characters can express the theme through their actions. The characters' actions show the reader what's really important. Winning a great battle, falling from grace for one's misdeeds, solving a mystery, or learning that revenge achieves little but harm.

The theme of a novel could **BEST** be described as
- A. its subject.
- B. the author.
- C. the point. *
- D. a thought.

(The definition is stated in the first sentence, though all the choices are in the passage. This question illustrates why it's not a good idea to look up and find the answer without reading.)

While ___ is a topic for a novel, the theme might be ___.
- A. war ... it is useless *
- B. man ... his thoughts
- C. lessons ... learning
- D. home ... is a building

(Choice A best illustrates how the theme is often the view of the author and/or main character about the topic.)

Which saying is **LEAST** likely to be the theme of a novel?
- A. Whatever you can conceive and believe, you can achieve.
- B. The journey of a thousand miles begins with a single step.
- C. Home is where the heart is.
- D. A stitch in time saves nine. *

(D really doesn't make sense. The others could be story lessons, or themes.)

Theme Thinking

DIRECTIONS: Briefly consider each of the themes listed plus one more of your choice and jot ideas for a simple storyline that could make each point. You'll have only a few minutes to do this, so think fast!

True happiness –

Self-discovery –

War and peace –

Dealing with prejudice –

What it means to be a hero –

What it means to be a survivor –

Revenge –

The big mystery –

Responsibility to others and society –

Love of family or friends –

True romantic love –

Dealing with despair –

Justice for harm –

Fulfilling a dream –

©InspirEd Educators, Inc.

Isn't It Ironic?

Springboard:
>   Students should study the "What's So Funny?" cartoons
>   and complete the handout as directed.
>   *(Both exemplify irony as defined below.)*

Objective: Students will be able to describe the types of irony and how its use can enhance characters or the storyline in a novel.

Materials: What's So Funny? (Springboard handout)
The Irony of It All (handout)
Is It or Isn't It Ironic? (2-page handout)
Seek and Ye May Find (handout)

Terms to Know: **irony** - contrast between what would be expected and what is actually said or done

Procedure:

· During discussion of the Springboard, introduce the term "irony" and have the student(s) explain how each cartoon exemplifies irony and why. *(The opposite of what should happen does. The dog is getting "wet" by the hydrant, and the reporter who's looking for a comment with all the cameras running gets a burp instead.)* Explain that <u>in this lesson the student(s) will learn more about irony</u>.

· Distribute "The Irony of It All" and the "Is It or Isn't It Ironic?" handouts. Read together or have the student(s) read the information about irony, and then have them work individually, in pairs, or groups to read the situations and decide which are ironic or not and why, and identify which types of irony are presented.

· Have them share their answers and discuss. During discussion of the last situation about The Wizard of Oz, explain that <u>the book is actually full of irony</u> and have the student(s) try to identify some. *(The scarecrow wants a brain but is already smart; the lion wants courage but saves the day; the tin man wants a heart but is the most emotional of the characters; Dorothy happens to kill the identical twin of the wicked witch; the "great and powerful" wizard is a puny, little guy; etc.)* In follow up have the student(s) explain why authors would use irony in their writing. *(Irony can add humor, tension, twists and turns to a story, etc. making a novel more interesting.)*

· **EXTENSION:** Play or read the lyrics to "Isn't It Ironic" by Alanis Morissette and have the student(s) decide which situations in the song they think actually are irony and which are not.

· Finally, distribute the "Seek and Ye May Find" organizer for the student(s) to use with their own novel.

78   ©InspirEd Educators, Inc.

What's So Funny?

DIRECTIONS: Explain the humor in each cartoon. Then answer the questions below.

In what way is the humor of these two cartoons similar? Explain your ideas. _____
_____
_____
_____
_____

Can you think of other similar situations? If so, jot your ideas here: _____
_____
_____
_____
_____

©InspirEd Educators, Inc.

The Irony of It All

"Seeing a kid eating an ice cream cone would be perfectly ordinary, but if you saw me out on the street somewhere, well ... that's irony!"

Irony is the contrast between whatever is normal, expected, or what appears to be and what actually is – seen, said, or done. That's a mouthful, but basically something is ironic if it means the opposite of what you think it should mean. Or it's ironic if what happens is exactly the opposite of what you would expect. (I must note that there is at least a hint of irony in your learning about it from an ice cream cone.) Often irony is funny, but just as often it isn't. You see, the thing is that irony can come in different forms.

<u>Verbal irony</u> is the difference between what is said and what is actually meant. Sarcastic remarks like, "Way to go, Michael Jackson," to an adolescent dancing clumsily, is cruel. Of course sarcasm isn't always cruel. Saying "I didn't even know you could read" to your best friend who just won the state Spelling Bee would likely be a friendly joke and taken kindly. Both comments are verbal irony.

<u>Situational irony</u> is something that happens, which is the opposite of what is expected or intended: the twist at the end of a story. Situational irony can be funny or tragic. In *Romeo and Juliet* the twist results in the death of both main characters. An author may build up a story letting the reader think one character is going to kill or be killed. But then the unexpected occurs – the twist – and the reader is left thinking, "Wow, I didn't see that coming at all!" That's situational irony.

Life is full of situational irony; you just have to look for it. The school bully breaks down in tears when an older child picks on him. A thief's house where he stores all the loot gets robbed. A pickpocket gets her pocket picked. The class know-it-all gets the worst grade on a test. It happens, and when it does, it's ironic. The Titanic, a ship billed as "unsinkable" sinks.

The last form of irony, <u>dramatic irony</u>, occurs when the audience or reader knows more than the characters know, so it is the difference between what the character THINKS is true and what the reader KNOWS is going to happen. The point of this type of writing is to build up tension in the reader, wondering how the character will find out the truth. What will she say? How will he react?

Mystery writers commonly use this device in their writing. The reader knows the husband wants to murder his wife; knows the knife is in the drawer of the nightstand. Still unaware, the soon-to-be victim climbs the steps to get ready for bed. The reader waits, wanting to warn the woman, tell her to run, but ...

In general, dramatic irony takes a serious tone, but can be funny as well if the reader is in on the joke. A husband keeps his wife out doing errands all day on her birthday with the promise of a lovely, relaxing evening at home: a steak dinner and candlelight. But when they finally get home after an exhausting day, she is startled by a houseful of guests: "SURPRISE!"

IS IT OR ISN'T IT IRONIC?

DIRECTIONS: Write whether each situation **is** or **isn't** ironic in the blank. Then if it is irony, explain which type and why. If it isn't, explain why not.

_____ "An old man turns ninety-eight. He wins the lottery and dies the next day."

_____ A family is hosting a picnic, and the wife sends her husband out for plastic forks. When he gets to the store, there are spoons and knives, but the folks are sold out.

_____ "You've really made a mess of things!" said in congratulations to a graduate at the top of her class.

_____ A man gets caught in a traffic jam when he's already running late for work.

_____ A group of firefighters are cooking dinner in the station during a big football game. As they are watching TV, cheering on their team, a pan catches fire and the station burns down.

_____ A soldier serves in a foreign war for two years. When he goes home, he is sitting out on his front porch and is shot by a stray bullet and killed.

_____ An average-looking guy asks out a beautiful woman and she turns him down.

_____ A very handsome man is standing by a rather plain-looking woman and starts making small talk. She simply says, "Excuse me," and walks away.

_____ A restaurant called "Hard Times Cafe" closes down during a bad economic period.

©InspirEd Educators, Inc.   81

_____ A mom is tired of picking up her son's dirty clothes that he just drops wherever he takes them off. She says, "Would Milord please inform his humble servant when he wishes to have his clothes put in the hamper?"

_____ A man hits a pothole and gets a flat tire while driving to an important business meeting and comments to himself, "Exactly what I needed."

_____ A woman with a fear of flying wins an award but has to fly cross-country to receive it. Her first flight ever; the plane crashes and she is killed.

_____ During the whole movie the reader thinks the sickly sister is going to die, but the healthy one dies in a freak accident.

_____ Two friends go out to karaoke one evening. One gets up and totally butchers her song, and her friend says, "Your Grammy Award awaits."

_____ Bill Gates, a multi-BILLIONAIRE and one of the richest people in the world, wins a Sweepstakes. The Prize Patrol goes to his door with a big cardboard check for a million dollars.

_____ A sixteen-year-old boy has a big date on Friday night and wants to borrow his dad's car for it, but the car breaks down on Thursday and has to be put in the shop.

_____ A teen in a slasher film runs into the closet in her bedroom to hide from the crazed murderer who is in the closet awaiting her going to bed.

_____ Dorothy spends the entire book, The Wizard of Oz, trying to get back home to Kansas. Then it turns out in the end that she had the ability to go home at any time using her ruby slippers.

IS IT OR ISN'T IT IRONIC? - SUGGESTIONS FOR ANSWERS

NOTE: Though suggested answers are provided, others are certainly acceptable if they are explained and well-reasoned.

_Is_ "An old man turns ninety-eight. He wins the lottery and dies the next day." *This would be situational irony, particularly if the man had been poor all his life.*

Isn't A family is hosting a picnic, and the wife sends her husband out for plastic forks. When he gets to the store, there are spoons and knives, but the folks are sold out. *A store being sold out of an item is an everyday occurrence. Though the husband may be inconvenienced and have to go elsewhere, the situation is not completely UNEXPECTED.*

_Is_ "You've really made a mess of things!" said in congratulations to a graduate at the top of her class. *This is verbal irony, since the meaning is the opposite of what is said.*

Isn't A man gets caught in a traffic jam when he's already running late for work. *Leaving late for work and getting caught in traffic wouldn't be irony. It would not only be EXPECTED to hit traffic on the way to work, it would be LIKELY especially since the driver left home late. In fact, he probably leaves early specifically to avoid the traffic.*

_Is_ A group of firefighters are cooking dinner in the station during a big football game. As they are watching TV, cheering on their team, a pan catches fire and the station burns down. *This would be situational irony since the job of the firefighters is to save buildings from fires, and the opposite occurs.*

_Is_ A soldier serves in a foreign war for two years. When he goes home, he is sitting out on his front porch and is shot by a stray bullet and killed. *This is also situational irony. The soldier spent two years in the line of fire and wasn't hurt in a situation in which people are expected to die. He's killed in an UNEXPECTED place; his front porch is far more likely to be safe than war.*

Isn't An average-looking guy asks out a beautiful woman and she turns him down. *There's nothing unexpected about this situation.*

Isn't A very handsome man is standing by a rather plain-looking woman and starts making small talk. She simply says, "Excuse me," and walks away. *This could actually go either way depending upon the surrounding circumstances. Had the guy been boasting how easy it is for him to get dates, it would be. However as stated, even though the man is handsome and the woman isn't, he's still a stranger. She could be married, might not have heard him, have something else on her mind, etc.*

_Is_ A restaurant called "Hard Times Cafe" goes out of business during a bad economic period. *This could arguably just be coincidence, but the name does suggest situational irony. It could be dramatic if the reader "saw it coming."*

©InspirED Educators, Inc.

__Is__ A mom is tired of picking up her son's dirty clothes that he just drops wherever he takes them off. She says, "Would Milord please inform his humble servant when he wishes to have his clothes put in the hamper?" *This is sarcasm, or verbal irony. It's the mom's way of telling the kid to pick up his own clothes.*

__Both__ A man hits a pothole and gets a flat tire while driving to an important business meeting and comments to himself, "Exactly what I needed." *This is more of a bad luck situation. A driver could hit a pothole and get a flat tire anytime. This flat just came at a bad time. Although, what he says could be considered verbal irony.*

__Is__ A woman with a fear of flying wins an award but has to fly cross-country to receive it. Her first flight ever; the plane crashes and she is killed. *This is situational irony. She never flew because she was afraid, but the one time she finally did happened to be a flight that crashed. The fact that her fear had kept her from flying up to this point creates the irony. Otherwise it would just be tragic.*

__Is__ During the whole movie the audience thinks the sickly sister is going to die, but the healthy one dies in a freak accident. *This is situational irony, since the audience DOESN'T KNOW what's going to happen.*

__Is__ Two friends go out to karaoke one evening. One gets up and totally butchers her song, and her friend says, "Your Grammy Award awaits." *The singer's friend is being sarcastic, so this is an example of verbal irony.*

__Is__ Bill Gates, a multi-BILLIONAIRE and one of the richest people in the world, wins a Sweepstakes. The Prize Patrol goes to his door with a big cardboard check for a million dollars. *The situation is ironic because Bill Gates already has more money than he needs. It's situational irony since no one knew ahead of time. If the reader or viewer knew, it would be dramatic irony.*

__Isn't__ A sixteen-year-old boy has a big date on Friday night and wants to borrow his dad's car for it, but the car breaks down on Thursday and has to be put in the shop. *There is nothing odd or unexpected about the fact that the teenager didn't get to use the car. Things like this just happen, and they happen all the time.*

__Is__ A teen in a slasher film runs into the closet in her bedroom to hide from the crazed murderer who is in the closet awaiting her going to bed. *This is most likely an example of dramatic irony. It is common in such movies for the viewer to know the killer is hiding in the closet. If not, it would be situational irony.*

__Is__ Dorothy spends the entire book, The Wizard of Oz, trying to get back home to Kansas. Then it turns out in the end that she had the ability to go home at any time using her ruby slippers. *This is situational, since the reader doesn't know until Dorothy does that the slippers can take her home.*

84   ©InspirEd Educators, Inc.

SEEK AND YE MAY FIND

DIRECTIONS: Find any examples of irony that you can in your novel and record them in the appropriate place on the organizer, explaining why each is ironic.

VERBAL IRONY

SITUATIONAL IRONY

DRAMATIC IRONY

Tying Up Loose Ends

Springboard:
Students should read "A Rave Review?" and answer the questions.

Objective: The student will be able to analyze information collected throughout the unit to write a novel review.

Materials: A Rave Review? (Springboard handout)
A Novel Review (handout)

Terms to know: **review** - a critical evaluation of a book, movie, event, product, etc.

Procedure:

- During discussion of the Springboard, make sure the student(s) understand that *the people who write reviews are not usually skilled in what they are evaluating. Food critics are usually not chefs, but they enjoy food and know what makes a meal good. Likewise book reviewers are not authors, but they read a great deal, understand literature, and know what they like.* Go on to explain that *in this lesson the student(s) will be guided through the process of reviewing the novel they read.*

- Distribute "A Novel Review" and review the requirements and directions. The student(s) should then work individually (unless more than one read the same novel) through the steps to create their book reviews.

- They should then either read or perform their reviews and evaluate their work using the rubric provided, noting what the reviewer(s) did particularly well as appropriate.

◇ ◇ A Rave Review? ◇ ◇

When most people think of reviews, they might envision a snooty food critic or guys arguing back and forth about movies, rating them with "two thumbs up or down or one each." TV and film often show scenes of actors or directors grabbing the newspaper to see what the critics thought of their plays, movies, or shows.

Anything can be reviewed, and a good review from almost any source certainly can't hurt! If the food critic raves about a restaurant, people will soon be flocking to have dinner there. Rave reviews fill theater and concert seats, too. But just as rave reviews can mean box office success for movies, gold records for singers, and long waits for new car delivery, a bad review can be crushing. Plays and restaurants close, movies go quickly to rental, and careers are ruined.

It is therefore very important for reviewers to think carefully about what they say or write. Respected reviewers guide buyers to the highest quality products, the best prices, and help people spend their entertainment dollars wisely. A good review provides important information, describing whatever is being reviewed and evaluating it fairly. It clearly states the reviewer's opinion and supports that view, giving specifics about what the reviewer did or did not like.

An author who publishes a new novel experiences much of the same **angst** as actors, chefs, and car dealers. If a book is reviewed well, its sales will surely reflect that; and of course the reverse is true. A good reviewer understands the impact his or her words may have and takes the time and care to look at many elements of the work in order to judge it fairly.

A review would **BEST** be described as a/an
- A. assessment.
- B. understanding.
- C. book.
- D. source.

Reviews are ___ because they affect ___.
- A. good … actors and directors
- B. rave … food and restaurants
- C. critical … entertainment dollars
- D. important … people's spending

The word "angst" in the last paragraph most nearly means
- A. calm.
- B. support.
- C. information.
- D. nervousness.

Which sentence does **NOT** state a requirement for a good book review?
- A. A good review should be fair and unbiased.
- B. It must tell the story clearly and completely.
- C. The reviewer should be honest and clear.
- D. It should provide and support an opinion.

It is **MOST** important that a book reviewer be
- A. an avid reader.
- B. a clear speaker.
- C. an excellent actor.
- D. a talented author.

©InspirEd Educators, Inc.

A Rave Review?
Answers & Explanations

When most people think of reviews, they might envision a snooty food critic or guys arguing back and forth about movies, rating them with "two thumbs up or down or one each." TV and film often show scenes of actors or directors grabbing the newspaper to see what the critics thought of their plays, movies, or shows.

Anything can be reviewed, and a good review from almost any source certainly can't hurt! If the food critic raves about a restaurant, people will soon be flocking to have dinner there. Rave reviews fill theater and concert seats, too. But just as rave reviews can mean box office success for movies, gold records for singers, and long waits for new car delivery, a bad review can be crushing. Plays and restaurants close, movies go quickly to rental, and careers are ruined.

It is therefore very important for reviewers to think carefully about what they say or write. Respected reviewers guide buyers to the highest quality products, the best prices, and help people spend their entertainment dollars wisely. A good review provides important information, describing whatever is being reviewed and evaluating it fairly. It clearly states the reviewer's opinion and supports that view, giving specifics about what the reviewer did or did not like.

An author who publishes a new novel experiences much of the same **angst** as actors, chefs, and car dealers. If a book is reviewed well, its sales will surely reflect that; and of course the reverse is true. A good reviewer understands the impact his or her words may have and takes the time and care to look at many elements of the work in order to judge it fairly.

A review would **BEST** be described as a/an
- A. assessment. *
- B. understanding.
- C. book.
- D. source.

(An assessment is an evaluation, which states an opinion about quality, ability, etc. and fully explains that opinion.)

Reviews are ___ because they affect ___.
- A. good … actors and directors
- B. rave … food and restaurants
- C. critical … entertainment dollars
- D. important … people's spending *

(The words must fill in both blanks and make sense. Choice D is MOST correct. C is somewhat true, but most people would not see entertainment as "critical.")

The word "angst" in the last paragraph most nearly means
- A. calm.
- B. support.
- C. information.
- D. nervousness. *

(The anxiety of actors running to the paper to read the reviews is because of the nervousness they felt about what the critics would say.)

Which sentence does **NOT** state a requirement for a good book review?
- A. A good review should be fair and unbiased.
- B. It must tell the story clearly and completely. *
- C. The reviewer should be honest and clear.
- D. It should provide and support an opinion.

(A review should not tell the WHOLE story, but briefly summarize and then evaluate it.)

It is **MOST** important that a book reviewer be
- A. an avid reader. *
- B. a clear speaker.
- C. an excellent actor.
- D. a talented author.

(B is important, but reading a great deal would offer a basis of comparison.)

©InspirEd Educators, Inc.

A NOVEL REVIEW

As a final project for this study of novels, you will review the one you read. Follow the steps below to complete the project. Your final review may be written or performed, but be sure to refer to the rubric as you work so you can focus on what is being evaluated.

1. Gather and review all of the organizers and notes you've taken about your novel throughout the unit.

2. Take time to consider all aspects of the novel, jotting notes as you do so:
   - What are the basic points of the book you want to include in a brief summary? Did you generally like the novel or not, and why?
   - What specifically did the author do well and/or poorly? Did he or she develop the characters, setting, and plot well? Are the round characters round and the flat ones less detailed? Were there places where he/she made effective use of figurative language, symbolism or irony?
   - Answer these questions and any others that seem appropriate.

3. Then use your notes to develop your evaluation and supporting reasons for it. Include specific information from the notes you've gathered throughout your reading and study.

4. Organize your ideas into a logical order for presentation and plan out and/or write your review. Keep in mind the final product as you work. If the review is to be written, take care to see that your writing flows, is clear, and correct. If it is to be performed, be sure it is organized and well-rehearsed before presenting it.

REVIEW RUBRIC

Use the following scale to evaluate your novel review:
4- Excellent   3- Good   2 – Fair   1- Poor   0 – Unacceptable

	Student Evaluation	Teacher Evaluation
Briefly summarizes work	_____	_____
Clear and supported opinion	_____	_____
Use of specifics to support view	_____	_____
Well-organized presentation	_____	_____
Interesting and helpful	_____	_____
Craftsmanship *	_____	_____

GRADE:

COMMENTS:

* Means correct spelling, grammar, and neatness for written review **OR** entertaining presentation, good eye contact, clearly spoken, well-rehearsed, etc. for performance.

©InspirEd Educators, Inc.

Reviewing Terms

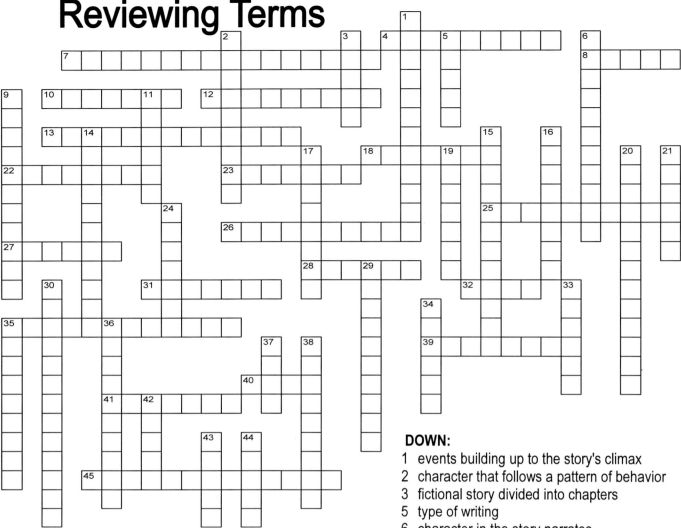

ACROSS:
- 4 information about a person's life
- 7 character development
- 8 "I could eat a horse!"
- 10 relating the arts and literature
- 12 person, animal, etc. in a story
- 13 invent or compose on the spot
- 18 made-up story
- 22 speech in writing
- 23 an author's intent for writer
- 25 person or thing that opposes the protagonist to create tension
- 26 the way a story's conflict works out
- 27 one thing representing something else
- 28 high point and turning point of a story
- 31 relating to sight, sound, taste, etc.
- 32 "feeling" the author creates
- 35 "some small snail snooped"
- 39 "He is a lion!"
- 40 friend or sidekick
- 41 place, time, surroundings of a story
- 45 clues to story events

DOWN:
- 1 events building up to the story's climax
- 2 character that follows a pattern of behavior
- 3 fictional story divided into chapters
- 5 type of writing
- 6 character in the story narrates
- 9 narrator is an outside observer
- 11 critical evaluation
- 14 main character
- 15 "Bam! Whack! Slap!"
- 16 story teller
- 17 problem or challenge
- 19 use of words to appeal to senses
- 20 triggers conflict in a story
- 21 guide for the protagonist
- 24 circumstance of use
- 29 background, interests, etc. that guides writers
- 30 events leading to the conflict's solution in a story
- 33 rectangular array or numbers, facts, etc.
- 34 "big as a house"
- 35 "May Shay want away."
- 36 story introduction and background
- 37 the main series of events in a story
- 38 major event; a turning point
- 42 broad idea or meaning
- 43 a quality or characteristic
- 44 contrast between what is expected and what actually is

90   ©InspirEd Educators, Inc.

Reviewing Terms Puzzle Answers

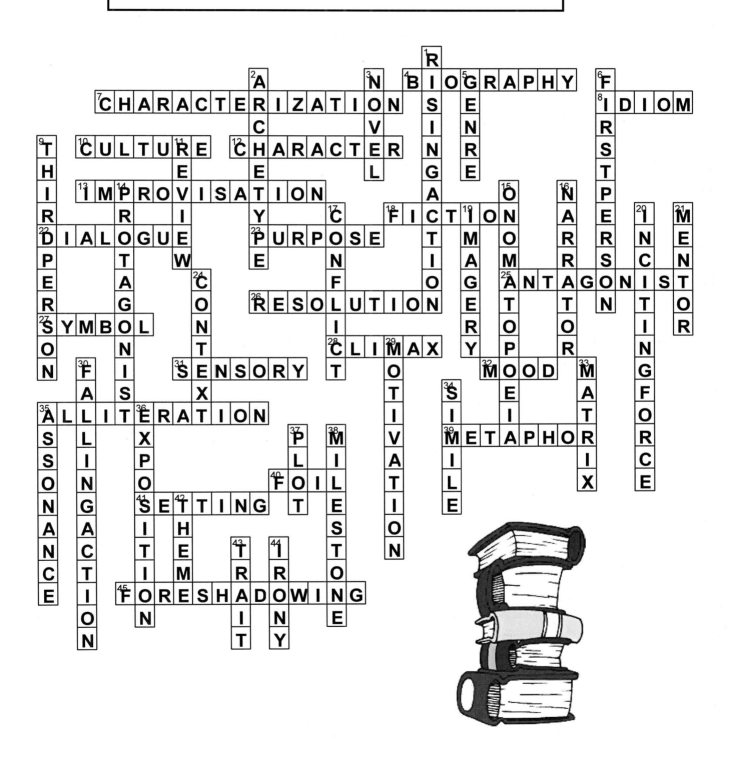

Novels (A)

Matching – Write the letter of the correct answer in the blank:
1. ___ fiction
2. ___ trait
3. ___ protagonist
4. ___ dialogue
5. ___ foil
6. ___ exposition
7. ___ symbol
8. ___ narrator
9. ___ milestone
10. ___ improvisation

A. storyteller
B. sidekick or friend
C. composing with little preparation time
D. quality or characteristic of a person
E. something that stands for something else
F. story with imaginary people and events
G. important event; turning point
H. speech; words in quotations
I. introduction and story background
J. the main character of a story

Give an example of each of the terms:
11. novel - _____
12. genre - _____
13. mood - _____
14. onomatopoeia - _____
15. setting - _____

Multiple Choice - Write the letter of the correct answer in the blank:
16. ____ Stories told in the ___ are usually more ___.
    A. first person …. serious
    B. first person …. personal
    C. third person …. one-sided
    D. third person …. fictional
17. ____ Round characters are all of the following **EXCEPT**
    A. complex.
    B. detailed.
    C. important to the story.
    D. bit players in a book.
18. ____ Which of these would **NOT** be a theme for a novel?
    A. "Love conquers evil."
    B. "The Princess and the Pea"
    C. "You'll never get ahead by lying."
    D. "Family is the most important thing."
19. ____ Which element of plot is the turning point in a story?
    A. inciting force
    B. rising action
    C. climax
    D. resolution

Fully answer the following question:
20. Explain at least two ways an author can develop a character in a story.

Skills for Forms A-C:

"Now the way that the book winds up is this: Tom and me found the money that the robbers hid in the cave, and it made us rich. We got six thousand dollars apiece -- all gold. It was an awful sight of money when it was piled up. Well, Judge Thatcher he took it and put it out at interest, and it fetched us a dollar a day apiece all the year round -- more than a body could tell what to do with. The Widow Douglas she took me for her son, and allowed she would civilize me; but it was rough living in the house all the time, considering how dismal regular and decent the widow was in all her ways; and so when I couldn't stand it no longer I lit out. I got into my old rags and my sugar-hogshead again, and was free and satisfied. But Tom Sawyer he hunted me up and said he was going to start a band of robbers, and I might join if I would go back to the widow and be respectable. So I went back. The widow she cried over me, and called me a __poor lost lamb,__ and she called me a lot of other names, too, but she never meant no harm by it."

Excerpt from Huckleberrry Finn, By Mark Twain

21. ____ All of these are true of the passage's point of view, **EXCEPT** it
    A. reveals the narrator's feelings.
    B. is told only in the first person.
    C. describes the story's setting.
    D. is likely a biased viewpoint.

22. ____ The underlined phrase is an example of
    A. a metaphor.   C. imagery.
    B. dialogue.   D. an idiom.

23. ____ The narrator in this passage is
    A. Judge Thatcher.   C. Huckleberry Finn.
    B. Tom Sawyer.   D. Widow Douglas.

PLOT DIAGRAM:

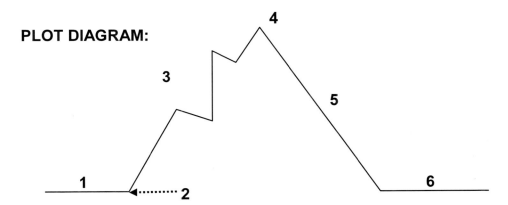

24. ____ In the plot diagram above, the resolution is labeled
    A. A1   B. 2   C. 4   D. 6

25. ____ The number **2** is the label for the story's
    A. exposition.   C. rising action.
    B. inciting force.   D. climax.

Novels (B)

Fill in the blanks with unit terms:
1. The _____ gave the reader hints about the coming murder.
2. Graduation and marriage are two major _____ of life.
3. The _____ offered the protagonist advice and support.
4. A story's _____ can be a character in it or an outside observer.
5. The _____ of the author's latest novel was sad and depressing.
6. "His family was his rock" is an example of a/an _____.
7. I read a great _____ of the new movie opening on Friday.
8. Authors' experiences often provide _____ for their stories.
9. _____ often includes made-up characters and situations.
10. The _____ left the characters living happily ever after.

Give an example of each of the terms:
11. genre: _____
12. trait: _____
13. archetype: _____
14. conflict: _____
15. simile: _____

Multiple Choice - Write the letter of the correct answer in the blank:
16. ____ Characters can be developed using all of these **EXCEPT**
    A. traits.
    B. imagery.
    C. dialogue.
    D. improvisation.
17. ____ Time, location and circumstances are all part of a novel's
    A. setting.
    B. conflicts.
    C. plot.
    D. characters.
18. ____ A clock could ____ a/an ____.
    A. review ..... plot
    B. symbolize ....life
    C. motivate .... reader
    D. divide ... novel
19. ____ Which of these statements is the **BEST** example of irony?
    A. An A student studies for a math test and aces it.
    B. A small town police station is robbed.
    C. An animal lover accidentally runs over a dog.
    D. A woman marries her best friend.

Fully answer the following question:
20. Explain three ways authors can use language to enhance a story.

Novels (C)

Complete the analogies with unit terms:
1. Simile is to as or like, as _____ is to neither.
2. Breed is to dog, as _____ is to literature.
3. Hints are to a guessing game, as _____ is to a story.
4. Rehearsals are to plays, as just doing it is to _____.
5. People are to real life, as _____ are to stories.
6. Flag is to a nation, as _____ is to what it represents.
7. Biography is to true lives, as _____ is to make-believe.
8. Setting is to a story, as _____ is to word usage.
9. Flat is to minor roles, as round is to the story's _____.
10. A grade is to a student, as a/an _____ is to an author.

Give an example of each of the terms:
11. idiom - _____
12. theme - _____
13. alliteration - _____
14. archetype - _____
15. assonance - _____

Multiple Choice - Write the letter of the correct answer in the blank:
16. ____ The protagonist is to the antagonist as
    A. a lioness is to her cubs.
    B. motivation is to purpose.
    C. an author is to a novel.
    D. a hero is to a villain.
17. ____ The story's ___ helped to enliven the ___.
    A. imagery … setting
    B. dialogue … narrator
    C. point-of-view … alliteration
    D. characterization … milestones
18. ____ The type of conflict exemplified by a character fighting cancer is
    A. man v. man.
    B. man v. society.
    C. man v. self.
    D. man v. nature.
19. ____ Which of these statements is the **BEST** example of irony?
    A. A student doesn't study for a test but still makes an A.
    B. Disgruntled citizens riot over the town's lawlessness.
    C. An animal lover takes in a stray while on vacation.
    D. A pediatrician's child comes down with the flu.

Fully answer the following question:
20. Explain at least three factors you think make a novel effective, and explain how.

©InspirEd Educators, Inc.

| | Novels Assessments
Suggestions for Answers |
|---|---|

Form A:
1. F
2. D
3. J
4. H
5. B
6. I
7. E
8. A
9. G
10. C

11. any novel they have read or know
12. mystery, romance, western, etc.
13. sad, excited, dreary, upbeat, etc.
14. Bam! Pow! Crash! etc.
15. forest, home, city, etc.
16. B
17. D
18. B
19. A
20. The author can describe the physical features, use dialogue, have the character interact with others, tell what he/she is thinking, etc.

Form B:
1. foreshadowing
2. milestones
3. mentor
4. narrator
5. mood
6. metaphor
7. review
8. motivation
9. fiction
10. resolution

11. mystery, romance, western, etc.
12. eye color, hair color, height, stubbornness, etc.
13. shrew, hero, outcast, mother, etc.
14. man vs. man, man vs. nature, man vs. self, etc
15. solid as a rock, quiet as a lamb, pretty as a picture, etc.
16. D
17. A
18. B
19. B
20. Answers will vary and include use of imagery, sensory character descriptions, irony, figurative language, etc.

Form C:
1. metaphor
2. genre
3. foreshadowing
4. improvisation
5. characters
6. symbol
7. fiction
8. context
9. protagonist
10. review

11. snake in the grass, foot the bill, eat a horse, etc.
12. coming of age, love conquers all, good triumphs over evil, etc.
13. six swimming swans, bugs black blood, etc.
14. shrew, hero, outcast, mother, etc.
15. May day, phone home, don't go on the boat, etc.
16. D
17. A
18. C
19. B
20. Answers will vary and include: good characterization, interesting plot, use of figurative language, irony, etc.

Skills forms A-C:
21. C
22. A
23. C
24. D
25. B

96   ©InspirEd Educators, Inc.

RESOURCES

www.orangeusd.k12.ca.us/yorba/literary_elements.htm - "Literary Elements," Yorba Middle School, 2009.

www.sdcoe.k12.ca.us/score/cyberguide.html - "Teacher Guides and Student Activities", SCORE Language Arts, 2009

mrbraiman.home.att.net/lit.htm - "Literary Devices," Jay Braiman, 2007.

www.scott.k12.va.us/jshipley/litel/LEPacket.htm - "Literary Elements," Scott County Public Schools, 2009.

www.learner.org/interactives/literature/read/charact1.html - "Creating Characters," Interactives - Literature, Annenberg Media, 2009.

www.literature.org/ - Literature.org, 2009.

galleryofwriting.org/ - "Your Guide to the National Gallery of Writing," National Council for the Teachers of English, 2009.

www.writingclasses.com/WritersResources/AskTheWriterDetail.php?ID=162 - "What's the Difference Between Flat and Round Characters," Ask the Writer, Gotham Writers' Workshop, 2009.

www.writingcorner.com/fiction/index.htm - "Fiction," Writing Corner.com, 2007.

www.cs.grinnell.edu/~simpsone/Connections/Fiction/index.html - Simpson, Eric, "Fiction," Connections: A Hypertext Resource for Literature, Grinnell College, 2009.

www.how-to-write-a-book-now.com/how-to-write-a-novel.html - "How to Write a Novel," How to Write a Book Now, Glen Strathy, 2008.

www.sarcasmsociety.com/irony - "Irony," Sarcasm Society, 2009.

www.writing.com/main/view_item/item_id/1581593 - "General Advice on Reviewing Novels," Writing.com, 21 X 20 Media, Inc., 2008.

www.unc.edu/depts/wcweb/handouts/review.html - "Book Reviews," The Writing Center, University of North Carolina at Chapel Hill, 2007.

©InspirEd Educators, Inc.

I Think: Thematic Units

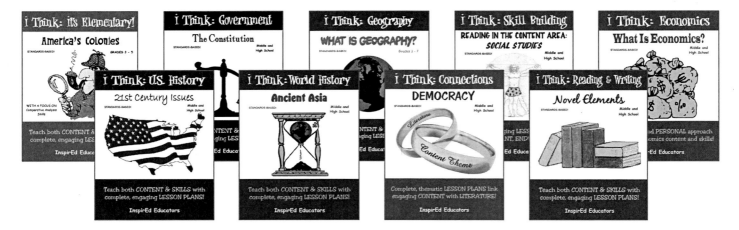

Some of our other **I Think** offerings include:

Series	Titles
I Think: It's Elementary!	America's Colonies, Revolution, Government, Economics, etc.
I Think: Government	Electing the President, Civic Participation, The Constitution, The Executive, Legislative, and Judicial Branches
I Think: U.S. History	Colonial America, American Revolution, Westward Expansion, The Civil War, Reconstruction Era, Problems & Progressives, The Modern Era, The African American Experience
I Think: World History	A wide variety of Ancient Civilizations units, Middle Ages, Renaissance, the World Wars, The Holocaust, etc.
I Think: Geography	What Is Geography?, U.S. Regions, World Geography by Region
I Think: Connections	Civilization, Democracy, Dictators, Ethnic Conflict, Indigenous People, Imperialism
I Think: Skill Building	Reading in the Content Area: *Social Studies* Research Skills
I Think: Reading & Writing	Poetry, Short Stories, Literary Themes, Novel Elements, Biographies, etc.
I Think: Economics	What Is Economics?, Personal Finance

We're adding more titles all the time.
Check our website for current listings!

www.inspirededucators.com